NEW YORK REVIEW BOOKS

POETS

ÁLVARO MUTIS (1923–2013) was born in Bogotá, Colombia. As a child he lived in Brussels, returning to Bogotá to complete his education. He lived in Mexico from 1956 until his death. Mutis's first poems were published in 1948, his first short stories in 1978, and his first novella, *The Snow of the Admiral*—the initial volume of the Maqroll series—in 1986. The complete *Adventures and Misadventures of Maqroll* is published by NYRB Classics.

CHRIS ANDREWS has translated books of prose fiction from Spanish and French by such authors as Kaouther Adimi, César Aira, Selva Almada, and Roberto Bolaño. He has been awarded the Valle-Inclán Prize and the French-American Foundation Translation Prize. He lives in Australia.

EDITH GROSSMAN (1936–2023) was a translator of poetry and prose by Gabriel García Márquez, Mario Vargas Llosa, Mayra Montero, Augusto Monterroso, Jaime Manrique, and Julián Ríos, among others.

ALASTAIR REID (1926–2014) was a poet, prose chronicler, translator, and traveler. Born in Scotland, he came to the United States in the early 1950s and lived in both Spain and Latin America for long spells. He was a constant translator of poetry from the Spanish language, in particular the work of Jorge Luis Borges and Pablo Neruda. He published more than forty books, among them a word book for children, *Ounce Dice Trice*, with drawings by Ben Shahn, which is available from New York Review Books.

Álvaro Mutis

Maqroll's Prayer
and Other Poems

TRANSLATED FROM THE SPANISH BY
CHRIS ANDREWS, EDITH GROSSMAN,
AND ALASTAIR REID

NYRB/POETS

 NEW YORK REVIEW BOOKS *New York*

THIS IS A NEW YORK REVIEW BOOK
PUBLISHED BY THE NEW YORK REVIEW OF BOOKS
207 East 32nd Street, New York, NY 10016
www.nyrb.com

Library of Congress Cataloging-in-Publication Data
Names: Mutis, Álvaro, author. | Andrews, Chris, translator. | Grossman,
  Edith, 1936–2023 translator. | Reid, Alastair, 1926–2014 translator. |
  Maqroll's prayer and other poems. | Maqroll's prayer and other poems.
  Spanish.
Title: Maqroll's prayer and other poems / Álvaro Mutis; translated from
  the Spanish by Chris Andrews, Edith Grossman, and Alastair Reid.
Description: New York City: New York Review Books, 2024. | Series: New
  York review books poets | Bilingual edition in English and Spanish. |
Identifiers: LCCN 2023040734 (print) | ISBN 9781590178744 (paperback) |
  ISBN 9781590178751 (ebook)
Subjects: LCSH: Mutis, Álvaro.—Translations into English. | LCGFT:
  Poetry.
Classification: LCC PQ8180.23.U8 A2 2024 (print) | LCC PQ8180.23.U8
  (ebook) | DDC 861/.64—dc23/eng/20230925
LC record available at https://lccn.loc.gov/2023040734
LC ebook record available at https://lccn.loc.gov/2023040735

ISBN 978-1-59017-874-4
Available as an electronic book; ISBN 978-1-59017-875-1

Cover and book design by Emily Singer

Printed in the United States of America on acid-free paper.
10 9 8 7 6 5 4 3 2 1

Contents

La creciente

Al amanecer crece el río, retumban en el alba los enormes troncos que vienen del páramo.

Sobre el lomo de las pardas aguas bajan naranjas maduras, terneros con la boca bestialmente abierta, techos pajizos, loros que chillan sacudidos bruscamente por los remolinos.

Me levanto y bajo hasta el puente. Recostado en la baranda de metal rojizo, miro pasar el desfile abigarrado. Espero un milagro que nunca viene.

Tras el agua de repente enriquecida con dones fecundísimos se va mi memoria.

Transito los lugares frecuentados por los adoradores del cedro balsámico, recorro perfumes, casas abandonadas, hoteles visitados en la infancia, sucias estaciones de ferrocarril, salas de espera.

Todo llega a la tierra caliente empujado por las aguas del río que sigue creciendo: la alegría de los carboneros, el humo de los alambiques, la canción de las tierras altas, la niebla que exorna los caminos, el vaho que despiden los bueyes, la plena, rosada y prometedora ubre de las vacas.

Voces angustiadas comentan el paso de cadáveres, monturas, animales con la angustia pegada en los ojos.

Los murciélagos que habitan la Cueva del Duende huyen lanzando agudos gritos y van a colgarse a las ramas de los guamos o a prenderse de los troncos de los cámbulos. Los espanta la presencia ineluctable y pasmosa del hediondo barro que inunda su morada. Sin dejar de gritar, solicitan la noche en actitud hierática.

El rumor del agua se apodera del corazón y lo tumba contra el viento. Torna la niñez...

¡Oh juventud pesada como un manto!

The Flood

As day breaks the river rises; huge trunks from the uplands crash and thump in the dawn.

Down on the back of the brown waters come ripe oranges, calves with mouths brutally agape, thatched roofs, screeching parrots startled by sudden eddies.

I get up and go down to the bridge. Propped against the reddish metal rail, I watch the motley parade pass by. I wait for a miracle that never occurs.

Drawn by the water abruptly enriched with prolific offerings, my memory sets out.

I pass through the haunts of the balsamic-cedar worshippers, explore perfumes, abandoned houses, hotels visited in childhood, filthy railway stations, waiting rooms.

It all comes down to the hot country, swept by the waters of the still-rising river: the coal miners' cheer, the smoke of the stills, the song of the high country, the mist that decorates the trails, the steam that rises from the oxen, the full, pink, promising udders of the cows.

Anguished voices remark on the passing of corpses, horses, animals with anguish fixed in their eyes.

Hurling their shrill cries, the bats that live in the Cave of the Spirit fly away to hang from the branches of guamo trees or attach themselves to the trunks of mountain immortelles. The irresistible, shocking presence of foul-smelling mud engulfing their roosts has driven them out. They strike hieratic poses, crying out all the while, beseeching night to come.

The water's murmur takes hold of the heart and flings it into the wind. Childhood returns...

Oh youth, heavy as a cloak!

La espesa humareda de los años perdidos esconde un puñado de cenizas miserables.

La frescura del viento que anuncia la tarde pasa velozmente por encima de nosotros y deja su huella opulenta en los árboles de la "cuchilla."

Llega la noche y el río sigue gimiendo al paso arrollador de su innúmera carga.

El olor a tierra maltratada se apodera de todos los rincones de la casa y las maderas crujen blandamente.

De cuando en cuando, un árbol gigantesco que viajara toda la noche anuncia su paso al golpear sonoramente contra las piedras.

Hace calor y las sábanas se pegan al cuerpo. Con el sueño a cuestas, tomo de nuevo el camino hacia lo inesperado en compañía de la creciente que remueve para mí los más escondidos frutos de la tierra.

1945–1947

The thick smoke of the lost years conceals a wretched handful of ashes.

The cool of the breeze that heralds the evening passes quickly overhead and leaves its sumptuous trace among the trees along the ridge.

Night comes, and the river groans on and on to the crushing rhythm of its measureless load.

An odor of abused earth occupies every corner of the house, and the timbers creak softly.

From time to time, a huge tree that must have journeyed all night announces its passage with a resonant blow to the stones.

It is hot, and sheets adhere to the body. Burdened with sleep, I set off once again for the unexpected, ushered by the flood that rummages for me among the earth's most hidden fruits.

1945–1947

[C.A.]

Tres imágenes

Para Luis Cardoza y Aragón

I

La noche del cuartel fría y señera
vigilia a sus hijos prodigiosos.
La arena de los patios se arremolina
y desaparece en el fondo del cielo.
En su pieza el Capitán reza las oraciones
y olvida sus antiguas culpas,
mientras su perro orina
contra la tensa piel de los tambores.
En la sala de armas una golondrina vigila
insomne las aceitadas bayonetas.
Los viejos húsares resucitan para combatir
a la dorada langosta del día.
Una lluvia bienhechora refresca el rostro
del aterido centinela que hace su ronda.
El caracol de la guerra prosigue su arrullo interminable.

2

Esta pieza de hotel donde ha dormido un asesino,
esta familia de acróbatas con una nube azul en las pupilas,
este delicado aparato que fabrica gardenias,
esta oscura mariposa de torpe vuelo,
este rebaño de alces,
han viajado juntos mucho tiempo
y jamás han sido amigos.
Tal vez formen en el cortejo de un sueño inconfesable
o sirvan para conjurar sobre mí
la tersa paz que deslíe los muertos.

Three Images

For Luis Cardoza y Aragón

1

The cold, solitary night of the barracks
watches over its prodigious sons.
Sand swirls up from the yards
and vanishes into the depths of the sky.
In his room the Captain says his prayers,
forgetting old trespasses
while his dog urinates
on the taut skins of the drums.
In the armory a sleepless swallow
keeps watch over the oiled bayonets.
The old hussars rise from the dead to fight
the golden locust of day.
A beneficent rain refreshes the face
of the sentinel numb with cold on his round.
The snail of war persists with its interminable lullaby.

2

This hotel room where a killer has slept,
this family of acrobats with a blue cloud in their pupils,
this delicate apparatus for making gardenias,
this dark butterfly with its bumbling flight,
this herd of elk,
have traveled together a long time
and have never been friends.
Perhaps they make up the retinue of some unspeakable dream
or serve to call down upon me
the shining peace that dissolves the dead.

3

Una gran flauta de piedra
señala el lugar de los sacrificios.
Entre dos mares tranquilos
una vasta y tierna vegetación de dioses
protege tu voz imponderable
que rompe cristales,
invade los estadios abandonados
y siembra la playa de eucaliptos.
Del polvo que levantan tus ejércitos
nacerá un ebrio planeta coronado de ortigas.

1947

3

A great stone flute
marks the sacrificial site.
Between two calm seas
a vast and tender growth of gods
shelters your imponderable voice
which shatters windows,
invades the abandoned stadiums,
and plants the beach with eucalypts.
The dust your armies raise will give birth
to a drunken planet crowned with thistles.

1947
[C.A.]

Programa para una poesia

Terminada la charanga, los músicos recogen adormilados sus instrumentos y aprovechan la última luz de la tarde para ordenar sus papeles.

Antes de perderse en la oscuridad de las calles, algunos espectadores dicen su opinión sobre el concierto. Unos se expresan con deliberada y escrupulosa claridad. Los hay que se refieren al asunto con un fervor juvenil que guardaron cuidadosamente toda la tarde, para hacerlo brillar en ese momento con un fuego de artificio en el crepúsculo. Otros hay que opinan con una terrible certeza y convicción, dejando entrever, sin embargo, en su voz, fragmentos del gran telón de apatía sobre el cual proyectan todos sus gestos, todas sus palabras.

La plaza se queda vacía, inmensa en la oscuridad sin orillas. El agua de una fuente subraya la espera y la ansiedad que con paulatina tersura se van apoderando de todo el ambiente.

A lo lejos comienza a oírse la bárbara música que se acerca. Del fondo más profundo de la noche surge este sonido planetario y rugiente que arranca de lo más hondo del alma las palpitantes raíces de pasiones olvidadas.

Algo comienza.

PROGRAMA

Todo está hecho ya. Han sonado todas las músicas posibles. Se han ensayado todos los instrumentos en su mezquino papel de solistas. A la gran noche desordenada y tibia que se nos viene encima hay que recibirla con un canto que tenga mucho de su esencia y que esté tejido con los hilos que se tienden hasta el más delgado filo del día que muere, con los

Program for Poetry

When the brass band finishes playing, the musicians, half-asleep, gather up their instruments and take advantage of the last light of evening to put their music in order.

Before they disappear into the dark streets, some spectators state their opinion of the concert. A few express themselves with deliberate and scrupulous clarity. Others refer to the matter with a youthful fervor they guarded carefully all afternoon in order to make it shine with burning artifice at that moment of twilight. Still others express their opinion with terrible certainty and conviction, yet in their voice allowing a vague sense of the fragments of a great curtain of apathy onto which they project all their gestures, all their words.

The square is left empty, immersed in unbounded darkness. The water in a fountain accentuates the expectation and apprehension that with gradual fluidity take possession of the surroundings.

In the distance barbaric music begins to be heard, drawing closer. From the most profound depths of the night this planetary bellow surges, tearing out the throbbing roots of forgotten passions from the deepest part of the soul.

Something commences.

PROGRAM

Now everything has been done. All possible music has been played. All the instruments have rehearsed their minor solo parts. The great disordered, indifferent night bearing down on us must be welcomed with a song that contains much of its essence and is woven with threads that extend to even the slimmest edge of the dying day, the tautest, longest

más tensos y largos hilos, con los más antiguos, con los que traen aún consigo, como los alambres del telégrafo cuando llueve el fresco mensaje matinal ya olvidado hace tanto tiempo.

Busquemos las palabras más antiguas, las más frescas y pulidas formas del lenguaje, con ellas debe decirse el último acto. Con ellas diremos el adiós a un mundo que se hunde en el caos definitivo y extraño del futuro.

Pero tiñamos esas palabras con la sombra provechosa y magnífica del caos. No del pequeño caos de entrecasa usado hasta ahora para asustar a los poetas-niños. No de esas pesadillas *ad hoc* producidas en serie para tratar ingenuamente de vacunarnos contra el gran desorden venidero.

No. Unjámonos con la desordenada especie en la que nos sumergiremos mañana.

Como los faraones, es preciso tener las más bellas palabras listas en la boca, para que nos acompañen en el viaje por el mundo de las tinieblas. ¿Que habrían hecho ellos con sus untuosas fórmulas cotidianas en tan terrible y eterno trance? Les hubieran pesado inútilmente retardando la marcha y desvistiéndola de grandeza.

Para prevenir cualquier posibilidad de que esto nos suceda ahora, es bueno poner al desnudo la esencia verdadera de algunos elementos usados hasta hoy con abusiva confianza y encerrados para ello en ingenuas recetas que se repiten por los mercados.

LA MUERTE

No inventemos sus aguas. Ni intentemos adivinar torpemente sus cauces deliciosos, sus escondidos remansos. De nada vale hacerse el familiar con ella. Volvámosla a su antigua y verdadera presencia. Venerémosla con las oraciones de antaño y volverán a conocerse sus rutas complicadas, tornará a

threads, the most ancient ones, the ones that still carry with them, like telegraph wires when it rains, the fresh message of morning now long forgotten.

Let us search for the most ancient words, the freshest and most polished forms of language, the final act should be spoken with them. With them we shall say goodbye to a world that sinks into the definitive, strange chaos of the future.

But let us darken those words with the auspicious, magnificent shadow of chaos. Not the small, domestic chaos used until now to frighten poet-children. Not those ad hoc nightmares produced en masse in an ingenuous attempt to inoculate us against the great disorder to come.

No. Let us anoint ourselves with the kind of disorder into which we shall sink tomorrow.

Like the pharaohs, we must have the most beautiful words ready in our mouths so they can accompany us on our journey to the world of darkness. What would they have done with their honeyed, quotidian formulas in so terrible and eternal a moment? They would have weighed them down to no avail, slowing their progress and stripping it of grandeur.

To prevent any possibility of this happening to us now, it is advisable to lay bare the true essence of certain elements used until today with abusive presumption and contained to that end in simple recipes replicated in every marketplace.

DEATH

Let us not invent her waters. Or clumsily attempt to divine her inviting riverbeds, her secret pools. Becoming her intimate is futile. Let us return her to her ancient and true existence. Let us revere her with the prayers of long ago, and her intricate courses will be known again, her dense tangle of blind

encantarnos su espesa maraña de ciudades ciegas en donde el silencio desarrolla su líquida especia. Las grandes aves harán de nuevo presencia sobre nuestras cabezas y sus sombras fugaces apagarán suavemente nuestros ojos. Desnudo el rostro, ceñida la piel a los huesos elementales que sostuvieron las facciones, la confianza en la muerte volverá para alegrar nuestros días.

EL ODIO

De todas las vendas con las cuales hemos tratado de curar sus heridas hagamos un sucio montón a nuestro lado. Que vibren los labios desnudos de la llaga al sol purificador del mediodía. Que los vientos desgarren la piel y se lleven pedazos de nuestro ser en su desordenado viaje por las extensiones. Sembremos la alta flor palpitante del odio. Arrojemos a los cuatro vientos su semilla. Con la cosecha en los brazos entraremos por las primeras puertas de blancos soportales.

No más falsificaciones del odio: el odio a la injusticia, el odio a los hombres, el odio a las formas, el odio a la libertad, no nos han dejado ver la gran máscara purificadora del odio verdadero, del odio que sella los dientes y deja los ojos fijos en la nada, a donde iremos a perdernos algún día. El dará las mejores voces para el canto, las palabras que servirán para sostener en lo más alto su arquitectura permanente.

EL HOMBRE

De su torpeza esencial, de sus gestos vanos y gastados, de sus deseos equívocos y tenaces, de su «a ninguna parte», de su clausurado anhelo de comunicarse, de sus continuos y risibles viajes, de su levantar los hombros como un simio hambriento,

cities where silence ripens her liquid spice. Great birds will again be present above our heads; their fleeting shadows will gently dim our eyes. Face bare, skin tight against the elemental bones that sustained her features, confidence in death will return to gladden our days.

HATRED

Let us make a filthy pile beside us of all the bandages we have used to try to heal his wounds. Let the naked lips of the gash vibrate in the purifying sun of midday. Let the winds tear at our skin and carry away pieces of our being in its disordered journey through vast expanses. Let us plant the tall palpitating flower of hatred. Let us cast its seed to the four winds. With the harvest in our arms we shall enter through the first doors of white porticos.

No more falsifications of hatred: hatred of injustice, hatred of men, hatred of forms, hatred of liberty, they have not allowed us to see the great purifying mask of true hatred, the hatred that clenches teeth and leaves eyes staring at nothingness, where we shall go to lose ourselves one day. It will offer the best voices for singing, the words that will serve to hold on high its permanent architecture.

MAN

From his essential dullness, his useless, worn-out gestures, his equivocal, tenacious desires, his "nowhere," his walled-in yearning to communicate, his continuous, laughable travels, his raising his shoulders like a hungry ape, his conventional, fearful laughter, his impoverished litany of passions, his prepared leaps without risk, his tepid, sterile entrails, from

de su risa convencional y temerosa, de su paupérrima letanía de pasiones, de sus saltos preparados y sin riesgo, de sus entrañas tibias y estériles, de toda esta pequeña armonía de entre-casa, debe hacer el canto su motivo principal.

No temáis el esfuerzo. A través de los siglos hay quienes lo han logrado hermosamente. No importa perderse por ello, tornarse extraño, separarse del camino y sentarse a mirar pasar la tropa con un espeso alcohol en la mirada. No importa.

LAS BESTIAS

¡Cread las bestias! Inventad su historia. Afilad sus grandes garras. Acerad sus picos curvados y tenaces. Dadles un itinerario calculado y seguro.

¡Ay de quienes no guardan un bestiario para enriquecer determinados momentos y para que nos sirva de compañía en el futuro!

Extendamos el dominio de las bestias. Que comiencen a entrar en las ciudades, que hagan su refugio en los edificios bombardeados, en las alcantarillas reventadas, en las torres inútiles que conmemoran fechas olvidadas. Entremos al reino de las bestias. De su prestigio depende nuestra vida. Ellas abrirán nuestras mejores heridas.

LOS VIAJES

Es menester lanzarnos al descubrimiento de nuevas ciudades. Generosas razas nos esperan. Los pigmeos meticulosos. Los grasientos y lampiños indios de la selva, asexuados y blandos como las serpientes de los pantanos. Los habitantes de las más altas mesetas del mundo, asombrados ante el temblor

all this small, inelegant harmony the principal motif of the song should be assembled.

Do not fear the effort. Throughout the centuries there are those who have accomplished it beautifully. It does not matter if you get lost, become strange, leave the road and sit down to watch the troops pass by with a dense alcohol in your gaze. It does not matter.

BEASTS

Create the beasts! Invent their history. Sharpen their great claws. Strengthen their curved, tenacious beaks. Give them a calculated, secure itinerary.

Woe to those who do not keep a bestiary to enrich determined moments and serve as our companions in the future!

Let us extend the dominion of the beasts. Let them begin to enter the cities, let them create their refuges in bombed-out buildings, blown-up bridges, useless towers that commemorate forgotten dates. Let us enter the kingdom of the beasts. Our lives depend on their authority. They will open our best wounds.

TRAVELS

It is necessary to throw ourselves into the discovery of new cities. Generous races await us. Shy Pygmies. Oily, hairless forest Indians, asexual and soft like the snakes in swamps. The inhabitants of the highest plateaus in the world, astonished at the trembling of snow. The weak inhabitants of frozen spaces. The herders of flocks. Those who have lived in the middle of the sea for centuries and whom no one

de la nieve. Los débiles habitantes de las heladas extensiones. Los conductores de rebaños. Los que viven en mitad del mar desde hace siglos y que nadie conoce porque siempre viajan en dirección contraria a la nuestra. De ellos depende la última gota de esplendor.

Faltan aún por descubrir importantes sitios de la Tierra: los grandes tubos por donde respira el océano, las playas en donde mueren los ríos que van a ninguna parte, los bosques en donde nace la madera de que está hecha la garganta de los grillos, el sitio en donde van a morir las mariposas oscuras de grandes alas lanudas con el color acre de la hierba seca del pecado.

Buscar e inventar de nuevo. Aún queda tiempo. Bien poco, es cierto, pero es menester aprovecharlo.

EL DESEO

Hay que inventar una nueva soledad para el deseo. Una vasta soledad de delgadas orillas en donde se extienda a sus anchas el ronco sonido del deseo. Abramos de nuevo todas las venas del placer. Que salten los altos surtidores no importa hacia dónde. Nada se ha hecho aún. Cuando teníamos algo andado, alguien se detuvo en el camino para ordenar sus vestiduras y todos se detuvieron tras él. Sigamos la marcha. Hay cauces secos en donde pueden viajar aún aguas magníficas.

Recordad las bestias de que hablábamos. Ellas pueden ayudarnos antes de que sea tarde y torne la charanga a enturbiar el cielo con su música estridente.

FIN

El pito sordo de un tren que cruza por regiones nocturnas. El humo lento de las fábricas que sube hasta el cielo color

knows because they always travel in a direction contrary to ours. The final drop of splendor depends on them.

There are still important places on earth to be discovered: the great pipes through which the ocean breathes, the beaches where the rivers that go nowhere come to die, the forests that give birth to the wood that the throats of crickets are made of, the place where dark butterflies, their huge wings downy with the acrid color of the dry grass of sin, go to die.

To seek and invent again. There is still time. Very little, it is true, but we must use it to our advantage.

DESIRE

A new solitude for desire must be invented. A vast, slim-edged solitude where the hoarse sound of desire can stretch out comfortably. Let us reopen all the veins of pleasure. Let the spurts leap high no matter in which direction. Nothing has been done yet. When we had something started, someone stopped on the way to order his clothing and everyone stopped behind him. Let us continue the march. There are dry riverbeds where magnificent waters still can travel.

Remember the beasts we have discussed. They can help us before it is too late and the marching band again disturbs the sky with its strident music.

ENDING

The muted whistle of a train that crosses regions of night. The slow smoke of factories rising to the apple-colored sky. The first lights that so strangely chill the streets. The hour when you wish to walk until you fall exhausted at the edge of night. The drowsy traveler in search of a cheap hotel.

manzana. Las primeras luces que enfrían extrañamente las calles. La hora cuando se desea caminar hasta caer rendido al borde de la noche. El viajero soñoliento en busca de un hotel barato. Los golpes de las ventanas que se cierran con un ruido de cristales retenidos por la pasta oleosa del verano. Un grito que se ahoga en la garganta dejando un sabor amargo en la boca muy semejante al de la ira o el intenso deseo. Los tableros de la clase con palabras obscenas que borrarán las sombras. Toda esta cáscara vaga del mundo ahoga la música que desde el fondo profundo de la noche parecía acercarse para sumergirnos en su poderosa materia.

Nada ocurre.

1952

The slam of windows that close with a sound of glass panes held by the oily paste of summer. A cry stifled in the throat that leaves a bitter taste in the mouth, like the taste of rage or intense desire. Blackboards in the classroom with obscene words that the shadows will erase. All this vague shell of the world suffocates the music that from the profound depths of night seemed to draw near to submerge us in its powerful substance.

Nothing occurs.

1952

[E.G.]

Oración de Maqroll

"Tu as marché par les rues de chair"
—René Crevel, *"Babylone"*

No está aquí completa la oración de Maqroll El Gaviero.
Hemos reunido sólo algunas de sus partes más salientes, cuyo
   uso cotidiano recomendamos a nuestros amigos como
   antídoto eficaz contra la incredulidad y la dicha inmotivada.

Decía Maqroll El Gaviero:

¡Señor, persigue a los adoradores de la blanda serpiente!
Haz que todos conciban mi cuerpo como una fuente inagot-
   able de tu infamia.
Señor, seca los pozos que hay en mitad del mar donde los
   peces copulan sin lograr reproducirse.
Lava los patios de los cuarteles y vigila los negros pecados
   del centinela. Engendra, Señor, en los caballos la ira de
   tus palabras y el dolor de viejas mujeres sin piedad.
Desarticula las muñecas.
Ilumina el dormitorio del payaso, ¡Oh Señor!
¿Por qué infundes esa impúdica sonrisa de placer a la esfinge
   de trapo que predica en las salas de espera?
¿Por qué quitaste a los ciegos su bastón con el cual rasgaban
   la densa felpa de deseo que los acosa y sorprende en las
   tinieblas?
¿Por qué impides a la selva entrar en los parques y devorar
   los caminos de arena transitados por los incestuosos, los
   rezagados amantes, en las tardes de fiesta?
Con tu barba de asirio y tus callosas manos, preside ¡Oh
   fecundísimo! la bendición de las piscinas públicas y el
   subsecuente baño de los adolescentes sin pecado.
¡Oh Señor! recibe las preces de este avizor suplicante y con-
   cédele la gracia de morir envuelto en el polvo de las

Maqroll's Prayer

"*Tu as marché par les rues de chair.*"
—René Crevel, *"Babylone"*

This is not a complete version of the prayer of Maqroll El
    Gaviero.
We have collected only some of its more salient elements,
    the daily use of which we recommend to our friends as a
    working antidote to incredulity and pure luck.

So spoke Maqroll El Gaviero:

Lord, persecute the worshippers of the pale serpent!
Let all conceive of my body as an inexhaustible fount of your
    infamy.
Lord, dry up those wells in the middle seas where fish copu-
    late without managing to reproduce.
Wash the patios of the barracks and watch over the black
    sins of the sentry. Engender in the horses, O Lord, the ire
    of your words and the pain of old women without faith.
Disconnect the dolls.
Bring light to the bedroom of the clown, O Lord.
Why do you infuse with that impudent smile of pleasure the
    face of the ragged prophet who preaches in waiting rooms?
Why did you take from the blind the stick with which they
    scratch away at the deep plush of the desire that surprises
    and harasses them in their twilight?
Why do you keep the jungle from invading the parks and
    swallowing the sand paths tracked by the incestuous, the
    trailing lovers on afternoons of fiesta?
With your Assyrian beard and your calloused hands, preside,
    Oh Most Fertile One, over the blessing of public swim-
    ming pools and the subsequent immersion of young peo-
    ple without sin.

ciudades, recostado en las graderías de una casa infame e
iluminado por todas las estrellas del firmamento.

Recuerda Señor que tu siervo ha observado pacientemente
las leyes de la manada. No olvides su rostro.

Amén.

O Lord, receive the prayers of this, your ever-watchful sup-
plicant; and grant him the grace of dying mantled in the
dust of cities, reclining on the altar of a house of ill-fame,
and illumined by all the stars in the firmament.

Remember, Lord, that your Servant has patiently obeyed the
laws of the multitude. Do not forget his face.

Amen.

[A.R.]

Los elementos del desastre

Una pieza de hotel ocupada por distracción o prisa, cuán pronto nos revela sus proféticos tesoros. El arrogante granadero "bersaglier" funambulesco, el rey muerto por los terroristas y cuyo cadáver despernancado en el coche se mancha precipitadamente de sangre, el desnudo tentador de senos argivos y caderas 1.900, la libreta de apuntes y los dibujos obscenos que olvidara un agente viajero. Una pieza de hotel en tierras de calor y vegetales de tierno tronco y hojas de plateada pelusa, esconde su cosecha siempre renovada tras el pálido orín de las ventanas.

2

No espera a que estemos completamente despiertos. Entre el ruido de dos camiones que cruzan veloces el pueblo, pasada la medianoche, fluye la música lejana de una humilde vitrola que lenta e insistente nos lleva hasta los años de imprevistos sudores y agrio aliento, al tiempo de los baños de todo el día en el río torrentoso y helado que corre entre el alto muro de los montes. De repente calla la música para dejar únicamente el bordoneo de un grueso y tibio insecto que se debate en su ronca agonía, hasta cuando el alba lo derriba de un golpe traicionero.

3

Nada ofrece de particular su cuerpo. Ni siquiera la esperanza de una vaga armonía que nos sorprenda cuando llegue la hora

The Elements of the Disaster

1

How soon a thoughtlessly or hastily occupied hotel room reveals its prophetic treasures. The arrogant, extravagant bersagliere grenadier; the king killed by terrorists, his body, legs akimbo in the car, suddenly covered in blood; the tempting nude with Argive breasts and 1900 hips; the notebook and the obscene drawings left, perhaps, by a traveling salesman. A hotel room in the land of heat and plants with tender trunks and silver-downed leaves conceals its ever-renewed collection behind the pale russet of its windows.

2

It does not wait until we are fully awake. Between one truck and the next speeding noisily through town after midnight, distant music flows from a humble phonograph, slowly, insistently taking us back to the years of unexpected sweats and sour breath, the time of daylong bathing in the swift, icy river that pours through the high wall of the mountains. Suddenly the music ceases, leaving only the drone of a big, listless insect, struggling in its hoarse death throes until dawn knocks it down with a treacherous blow.

3

At a glance, nothing special about her body. Not even the hope of a vague harmony that might take us by surprise when the time comes to undress. In her face, her countenance with

de desnudarse. En su cara, su semblante de anchos pómulos, grandes ojos oscuros y acuosos, la boca enorme brotada como la carne de un fruto en descomposición, su melancólico y torpe lenguaje, su frente estrecha limitada por la pelambre salvaje que desparrama como maldición de soldado. Nada más que su rostro advertido de pronto desde el tren que viaja entre dos estaciones anónimas; cuando bajaba hacia el cafetal para hacer su limpieza matutina.

4

Los guerreros, hermano, los guerreros cruzan países y climas con el rostro ensangrentado y polvoso y el rígido ademán que los precipita a la muerte. Los guerreros esperados por años y cuya cabalgata furiosa nos arroja a la medianoche del lecho, para divisar a lo lejos el brillo de sus arreos que se pierde allá, más abajo de las estrellas.

Los guerreros, hermano, los guerreros del sueño que te dije.

5

El zumbido de una charla de hombres que descansaban sobre los bultos de café y mercancías, su poderosa risa al evocar mujeres poseídas hace años, el recuerdo minucioso y pausado de extraños accidentes y crímenes memorables, el torpe silencio que se extendía sobre las voces, como un tapete gris de hastío, como un manoseado territorio de aventura... todo ello fue causa de una vigilia inolvidable.

its ample cheekbones: large, dark, liquid eyes; the great mouth swollen like the flesh of an overripe fruit; melancholic, drawling speech; a narrow strip of forehead bordered by the mop of hair tumbling forth like a soldier's curse. Nothing more than her face glimpsed unexpectedly from a train between two anonymous stations as she went down to the coffee plantation for her morning wash.

4

The warriors, brother, the warriors cross countries and climates with bloodied, dusty faces, and stiff movements that pitch them headlong into death. The warriors, awaited for years, whose raging cavalcade flings us onto the midnight bed, to spy the far-off gleam of their trappings, vanishing there, beneath the stars.

The warriors, brother, the dream warriors I told you about.

5

The buzz of men chatting as they take it easy on sacks of coffee and merchandise, their booming laughter as they recall women had years ago, the leisurely, detailed narration of curious accidents and memorable crimes, the awkward silence falling over the voices like a gray cloth of tedium, like a well-worn realm of adventure...all of this made for an unforgettable vigil.

6

La hiel de los terneros que macula los blancos tendones palpitantes del alba.

7

Un hidroavión de juguete tallado en blanda y pálida madera sin peso baja por el ancho río de corriente tranquila, barrosa. Ni se mece siquiera, conservando esa gracia blanca y sólida que adquieren los aviones al llegar a las grandes selvas tropicales. Qué vasto silencio impone su terso navegar sin estela. Va sin miedo a morir entre la marejada rencorosa de un océano de aguas frías y violentas.

8

Me refiero a los ataúdes, a su penetrante aroma de pino verde trabajado con prisa, a su carga de esencias en blanda y lechosa descomposición, a los estampidos de la madera fresca que sorprenden la noche de las bóvedas como disparos de cazador ebrio.

9

Cuando el trapiche se detiene y queda únicamente el espeso borboteo de la miel en los fondos, un grillo lanza su chillido desde los pozuelos de agrio guarapo espumoso. Así termina la pesadilla de una siesta sofocante, herida de extraños y urgentes deseos despertados por el calor que rebota sobre el dombo verde y brillante de los cafetales.

6

Calf bile that stains the throbbing white tendons of dawn.

7

A toy seaplane carved out of soft, pale, featherlight wood drifts on the broad river's gentle, muddy current. Not even rocking, it maintains that steady, white grace that planes assume when they reach the great tropical jungles. How vast the silence that determines its smooth and wakeless navigation. On it goes fearlessly to die in the spiteful swell of a cold and violent ocean.

8

I refer to the coffins, to their penetrating scent of hastily carpentered green pinewood, to their cargo of essences in soft and milky decomposition, to the cracking of the unseasoned timber, startling the night of the vaults like the shots of a drunken hunter.

9

When the sugar mill stops and there is only the viscid bubbling of the syrup in the depths, the shrill cry of a cricket starts up among the pots of tart, frothy cane juice. So concludes the nightmare of a stifling siesta, injured by strange and urgent desires that hatched in the heat reflected by the shiny green domes of the coffee plantations.

10

Afuera, al vasto mar lo mece el vuelo de un pájaro dormido en la hueca inmensidad del aire.

Un ave de alas recortadas y seguras, oscuras y augurales.

El pico cerrado y firme cuenta los años que vienen como una gris marea pegajosa y violenta.

11

Por encima de la roja nube que se cierne sobre la ciudad nocturna, por encima del afanoso ruido de quienes buscan su lecho, pasa un pueblo de bestias libres en vuelo silencioso y fácil.

En sus rosadas gargantas reposa el grito definitivo y certero. El silencio ciego de los que descansan sube hasta tan alto.

12

Hay que sorprender la reposada energía de los grandes ríos de aguas pardas que reparten su elemento en las cenagosas extensiones de la selva, en donde se crían los peces más voraces y las más blandas y mansas serpientes. Allí se desnuda un pueblo de altas hembras de espalda sedosa y dientes separados y firmes con los cuales muerden la dura roca del día.

10

Outside, the vast sea is rocked by the flight of a bird asleep in the hollow immensity of the air.

A bird whose wings are trimmed and sure, dark and augural.

Its closed and steady beak counts the years that are coming like a gray, sticky, violent tide.

11

Above the red cloud that looms over the nightbound city, above the laborious noise of those who are searching for their beds, a tribe of free animals passes in silent, easy flight.

The definitive, unerring cry resides in their pink throats. So high climbs the blind silence of those who have found their rest.

12

It has to be taken by surprise, the unhurried energy of the great dun-colored rivers that spread their element in the swampy expanses of the jungle, where the fiercest fish breed, along with the softest, tamest snakes. A tribe of tall women goes naked there, with silken backs and strong, spaced teeth for biting into the day's hard rock.

[C.A.]

La orquesta

1

La primera luz se enciende en el segundo piso de un café. Un sirviente sube a cambiarse de ropas. Su voz gasta los tejados y en su grasiento delantal trae la noche fría y estrellada.

2

Aparte, en un tarro de especias vacío, guarda un mechón de pelo. Un espeso y oscuro cadejo de color indefinido como el humo de los trenes cuando se pierde entre los eucaliptos.

3

Vestido de amianto y terciopelo, recorrió la ciudad. Era el pavor disfrazado de tendero suburbano. Cuántas historias se tejieron alrededor de sus palabras con un sabor de antaño como las nieves del poeta.

4

Así, a primera vista, no ofrecía belleza alguna. Pero detrás de su cuerpo temblaba una llama azul que arrastraba el deseo, como arrastran ciertos ríos metales imaginarios.

The Orchestra

1

On the second floor of a café, a first light comes on. A servant has gone up to change his clothes. His voice corrodes the tiled roofs, and in his greasy apron he brings the cold and starry night.

2

Out of the way, in an empty spice jar, he keeps a lock of hair. A thick, dark tangle the elusive color of train smoke dissipating among eucalypts.

3

Dressed in amianthus and velvet, he roamed the city. He was terror disguised as a suburban storekeeper. So many stories were woven around his words with a flavor of yesteryear like the snows the poet sang.

4

At first glance, there was nothing beautiful about her. But a blue flame flickered behind her body and drew desire, as certain rivers draw imaginary metals.

5

Otra luz vino a sumarse a la primera. Una voz agria la apagó como se mata un insecto. A dos pasos de allí, el viento golpeaba ciegas hojas contra ciegas estatuas. Paz del estanque... luz opalina de los gimnasios.

6

Sordo peso del corazón. Tenue gemido de un árbol. Ojos llorosos limpiados furtivamente en el lavaplatos, mientras el patrón atiende a los clientes con la sonrisa sucia de todos los días.

Penas de mujer.

7

En las aceras, el musgo dócil y las piernas con manchas aceitosas de barro milenario. En las aceras, la fe perdida como una moneda o como una colilla. Mercancías. Cáscara débil del hollín.

8

Polvo suave en la oreja donde brilla una argolla de pirata. Sed y miel de las telas. Los maniquíes calculan la edad de los viandantes y un hondo, innominado deseo surge de sus pechos de cartón. Mugido clangoroso de una calle vacía. Rocío.

5

Another light came to join the first. A sour voice extinguished it as one might kill an insect. Two steps away, the wind beat blind statues with blind leaves. The pond's tranquility... opaline gymnasium light.

6

The heart's dull weight. A tree's faint moan. Tear-filled eyes discreetly wiped over the sink, while the boss attends to clients with the dirty smile he wears every day.

Women's sorrows.

7

On the sidewalks, yielding moss, and legs with oily spots of thousand-year-old mud. On the sidewalks, faith lost like a coin or a cigarette butt. Merchandise. Frail shell of soot.

8

Soft dust in the ear adorned by a pirate's shining ring. Fabrics thirsting and honeyed. The mannequins calculate the ages of passersby, and a deep, unnamed desire wells up in their cardboard breasts. Strident bellowing of an empty street. Dew.

9

Como un loco planeta de liquen, anhela la firme baranda del colegio con su campana y el fresco olor de los laboratorios. Ruido de las duchas contra las espaldas dormidas.

Una mujer pasa y deja su perfume de cebra y poleo. Los jefes de la tribu se congregaron después de la última clase y celebran el sacrificio.

10

Una vida perdida en vanos intentos por hallar un olor o una casa. Un vendedor ambulante que insiste hasta cuando oye el último tranvía. Un cuerpo ofrecido en gesto furtivo y ansioso. Y el fin, después, cuando comienza a edificarse la morada o se entibia el lecho de ásperas cobijas.

9

As if for a mad planet of lichen, he longs for the school's sturdy banister, its bell, the fresh smell of its laboratories. The sound of the showers on sleepy backs.

A woman goes by trailing a scent of zebra and pennyroyal. Gathered after the final class, the chiefs of the tribe celebrate the sacrifice.

10

A life lost in futile attempts to find a smell or a house. A hawker who keeps trying until he hears the last tram. A body offered with a furtive, eager gesture. And then the end, when the construction of the dwelling begins or the bed with its scratchy blankets warms up.

[C.A.]

Amén

Que te acoja la muerte
con todos tus sueños intactos.
Al retorno de una furiosa adolescencia,
al comienzo de las vacaciones que nunca te dieron,
te distinguirá la muerte con su primer aviso.
Te abrirá los ojos a sus grandes aguas,
te iniciará en su constante brisa de otro mundo.
La muerte se confundirá con tus sueños
y en ellos reconocerá los signos
que antaño fuera dejando,
como un cazador que a su regreso
reconoce sus marcas en la brecha.

Amen

May death receive you
with all your dreams intact.
On your return from a furious adolescence,
at the start of the vacation you were never granted,
death will honor you with its first warning.
It will open your eyes to its great waters,
acquaint you with its steady breeze from another world.
Death will blend into your dreams
and recognize in them the signs
it left here and there in days gone by
as a homing hunter recognizes
his marks along the trail.

[C.A.]

Nocturno

Esta noche ha vuelto la lluvia sobre los cafetales.
Sobre las hojas de plátano,
sobre las altas ramas de los cámbulos,
ha vuelto a llover esta noche un agua persistente y
    vastísima
que crece las acequias y comienza a henchir los ríos
que gimen con su nocturna carga de lodos vegetales.
La lluvia sobre el cinc de los tejados
canta su presencia y me aleja del sueño
hasta dejarme en un crecer de las aguas sin sosiego,
en la noche fresquísima que chorrea
por entre la bóveda de los cafetos
y escurre por el enfermo tronco de los balsos gigantes.
Ahora, de repente, en mitad de la noche
ha regresado la lluvia sobre los cafetales
y entre el vocerío vegetal de las aguas
me llega la intacta materia de otros días
salvada del ajeno trabajo de los años.

Nocturne

Tonight the rain is coming down again on the coffee
    plantations.
On the banana leaves,
on the mountain immortelle's high branches,
an immense, relentless rain is falling again tonight,
filling the channels, beginning to swell
the rivers that moan
under their nocturnal load of vegetal sludge.
The rain is singing its presence
on the zinc roof, sending me far from sleep
to leave me where the restless waters rise
and chilly night drips
through the coffee trees' vault
and runs down the sick trunks of the giant balsa trees.
Suddenly, now, in the middle of the night
the rain is coming down again on the plantations,
and through the vegetal clamor of the waters
the substance of other days reaches me intact,
rescued from the alien grind of the years.

                                                    [C.A.]

Grieta matinal

Cala tu miseria,
sondéala, conoce sus más escondidas cavernas.
Aceita los engranajes de tu miseria,
ponla en tu camino, ábrete paso con ella
y en cada puerta golpea
con los blancos cartílagos de tu miseria.
Compárala con la de otras gentes
y mide bien el asombro de sus diferencias,
la singular agudeza de sus bordes.
Ampárate en los suaves ángulos de tu miseria.
Ten presente a cada hora
que su materia es tu materia,
el único puerto del que conoces cada rada,
cada boya, cada señal desde la cálida tierra
a donde llegas a reinar como Crusoe
entre la muchedumbre de sombras
que te rozan y con las que tropiezas
sin entender su propósito ni su costumbre.
Cultiva tu miseria,
hazla perdurable,
aliméntate de su savia,
envuélvete en el manto tejido con sus más secretos hilos.
Aprende a reconocerla entre todas,
no permitas que sea familiar a los otros
ni que la prolonguen abusivamente los tuyos.
Que te sea como agua bautismal
brotada de las grandes cloacas municipales,
como los arroyos que nacen en los mataderos.
Que se confunda con tus entrañas, tu miseria;
que contenga desde ahora los capítulos de tu muerte,
los elementos de tu más certero abandono.

Morning Cleft

Fathom your misfortune,
sound it out, know its most hidden recesses.
Oil the machinery of your misfortune,
set it on your path, use it to make your way,
and knock on every door
with the white cartilage of your misfortune.
Compare it with the misfortunes of others
and carefully measure the shock of its differences,
the singular sharpness of its edges.
Bear in mind at all times
that its substance is your substance,
the only port where you know each roadstead,
each buoy, each signal from the warm land
where you go ashore to reign like Crusoe
among the multitude of shadows
that brush past, that you bump into
without understanding their aims and ways.
Cultivate your misfortune,
make it durable,
nourish yourself with its sap,
wrap yourself in a cloak woven from its most secret threads.
Learn to tell it from all the rest;
don't let it become familiar to others
or allow your people to prolong it unduly.
May it be like baptismal water for you
sprung from the great municipal sewers,
like streams that rise in slaughter yards.
May your misfortune melt into your entrails;
may it contain even now the chapters of your death,
the elements of your surest abandonment.
Never leave your misfortune aside,

Nunca dejes de lado tu miseria,
así descanses a su vera
como junto al blanco cuerpo
del que se ha retirado el deseo.
Ten siempre lista tu miseria
y no permitas que se evada por distracción o engaño.
Aprende a reconocerla hasta en sus más breves signos:
el encogerse de las finas hojas del carbonero,
el abrirse de las flores con la primera frescura de la tarde,
la soledad de una jaula de circo varada en el lodo
del camino, el hollín de los arrabales,
el vaso de latón que mide la sopa en los cuarteles,
la ropa desordenada de los ciegos,
las campanillas que agotan su llamado
en el solar sembrado de eucaliptos,
el yodo de las navegaciones.
No mezcles tu miseria en los asuntos de cada día.
Aprende a guardarla para las horas de tu solaz
y teje con ella la verdadera,
la sola materia perdurable
de tu episodio sobre la tierra.

but rest on its verge
as beside the white body
from which desire has withdrawn.
Keep your misfortune ready at all times,
and don't be distracted or tricked into letting it slip away.
Learn to recognize even its most fleeting signs:
a shrug of the calliandra's delicate leaves,
the opening of flowers in the first cool of evening,
the solitude of a circus cage stranded in the mud
of a road, the soot of the slums,
the tin cup that doles out soup in the barracks,
the untidy clothing of the blind,
the hand bells that exhaust their call
on the lot planted with eucalypts,
the iodine of ocean voyages.
Don't mix your misfortune with everyday business.
Learn to keep it for the hours of your solace,
and weave from it the true,
the only lasting substance
of your episode on earth.

[C.A.]

"Un bel morir"

De pie en una barca detenida en medio del río
cuyas aguas pasan en lento remolino
de lodos y raíces,
el misionero bendice la familia del cacique.
Los frutos, las joyas de cristal, los animales, la selva,
reciben los breves signos de la bienaventuranza.
Cuando descienda la mano
habré muerto en mi alcoba
cuyas ventanas vibran al paso del tranvía
y el lechero acudirá en vano por sus botellas vacías.
Para entonces quedará bien poco de nuestra historia,
algunos retratos en desorden,
unas cartas guardadas no sé dónde,
lo dicho aquel día al desnudarte en el campo.
Todo irá desvaneciéndose en el olvido
y el grito de un mono,
el manar blancuzco de la savia
por la herida corteza del caucho,
el chapoteo de las aguas contra la quilla en viaje,
serán asunto más memorable que nuestros largos abrazos.

"Un bel morir"

Upright in a boat, stilled in the middle of a river
whose waters flow past in a slow eddying
of mud and roots,
the missionary blesses the chief's family.
Fruit, glass beads, animals, and jungle
all receive the succinct signs of blessing.
When the hand descends,
I will have died in my bedroom
whose windows rattle when the tram passes
and the milkman comes back in vain for his empty bottles.
By then not much of our story will be left—
some pictures in disarray,
some letters hidden somewhere or other,
what was said that day you went naked in the country.
All that will keep fading away to oblivion,
and a monkey's chatter,
the whitish trickle of sap
from the wounded bark of the rubber tree,
the slap of water against the moving keel,
will be remembered more than our long lovemaking.

[A.R.]

Cita

In memoriam J.G.D.

Bien sea a la orilla del río que baja de la cordillera
golpeando sus aguas contra troncos y metales dormidos,
en el primer puente que lo cruza y que atraviesa el tren
en un estruendo que se confunde con el de las aguas;
allí, bajo la plancha de cemento,
con sus telarañas y sus grietas
donde moran grandes insectos y duermen los murciélagos;
allí, junto a la fresca espuma que salta contra las piedras;
allí bien pudiera ser.
O tal vez en un cuarto de hotel,
en una ciudad a donde acuden los tratantes de ganado,
los comerciantes en mieles, los tostadores de café.
A la hora de mayor bullicio en las calles,
cuando se encienden las primeras luces
y se abren los burdeles
y de las cantinas sube la algarabía de los tocadiscos,
el chocar de los vasos y el golpe de las bolas de billar;
a esa hora convendría la cita
y tampoco habría esta vez incómodos testigos,
ni gentes de nuestro trato,
ni nada distinto de lo que antes te dije:
una pieza de hotel, con su aroma a jabón barato
y su cama manchada por la cópula urbana
de los ahítos hacendados.
O quizá en el hangar abandonado en la selva,
a donde arrimaban los hidroaviones para dejar el correo.
Hay allí un cierto sosiego, un gótico recogimiento
bajo la estructura de vigas metálicas
invadidas por el óxido
y teñidas por un polen color naranja.
Afuera, el lento desorden de la selva,

Appointment

In memoriam J.C.D.

Perhaps by the river that comes down from the cordillera
hurling its waters at trunks and sleeping metal,
on the first bridge that spans it, crossed by the train
raising a din that swells the waters' roar;
there, beneath the cement slab
with its spiderwebs and crevices
where big insects lodge and bats hang asleep;
there, beside the cool foam spattering the rocks;
that could well be the place.
Or perhaps a hotel room,
in a city frequented by livestock dealers,
honey traders, coffee roasters.
When the bustle is peaking in the streets,
with the first lights coming on,
the brothels opening
and the clamor of the record players rising from the bars
along with the clinking of glasses and the clacking of
    billiard balls,
that would be a suitable time for the appointment,
without any inconvenient witnesses,
or anyone we know,
or anything other than what I told you:
a hotel room, with its smell of cheap soap,
its bed stained by the urban coition
of sated landowners.
Or perhaps that disused hangar in the jungle,
where seaplanes once pulled in to deliver mail.
A certain tranquility reigns there, a gothic contemplation
beneath the lattice of metal struts
eaten away by rust
and stained by an orange pollen.

su espeso aliento recorrido
de pronto por la gritería de los monos
y las bandadas de aves grasientas y rijosas.
Adentro, un aire suave poblado de líquenes
listado por el tañido de las láminas.
También allí la soledad necesaria,
el indispensable desamparo, el acre albedrío.
Otros lugares habría y muy diversas circunstancias;
pero al cabo es en nosotros
donde sucede el encuentro
y de nada sirve prepararlo ni esperarlo.
La muerte bienvenida nos exime de toda vana sorpresa.

Outside, the jungle's slow disorder,
its dense breath suddenly shot through
with monkey racket
and gangs of fat, quarrelsome birds.
Inside, mellow air laden with lichen spores
striped by the clanging iron sheets.
Here too the necessary solitude,
the essential neglect, the bitter volition.
There may be other places and quite different circum-
    stances,
but in the end it is within us
that the encounter occurs,
and preparing or awaiting it is futile.
Welcome death relieves us of any vain surprise.

[C.A.]

Cita

Y ahora que sé que nunca visitaré Estambul,
me entero que me esperan en la calle de Shidah Kardessi,
en el cuarto que está encima de la tienda del oculista.
Un golpe de aguas contra las piedras de la fortaleza,
me llamará cada día y cada noche
hasta cuando todo haya terminado.
Me llamará sin otra esperanza
que la del azar agridulce
que tira de los hilos neciamente
sin atender la música
ni seguir el asunto en el libreto.
Entretanto, en la calle de Shidah Kardessi
tomo posesión de mis asuntos
mientras se extiende el tiempo
en ondas crecientes y sin pausa
desde el cuarto que está encima
de la tienda del oculista.

Appointment

Now that I know that I'll never visit Istanbul,
I realize I'm expected, in that street, Shidah Kardessi,
in the room that sits above the oculist's workshop.
The splash of water on the stones of the fortress
will summon me, every day and every night, until
the very end of time.
It will summon me, with no more expectation
than that of a bittersweet fingering
of the strings, idly, carelessly,
not expecting any music
or following any libretto.
Meanwhile, in that street, Shidah Kardessi,
I attend to all my obligations
while time unwinds
in gathering waves, never-ending,
from that room, that room that sits above
the workshop of the oculist.

[A.R.]

Cada poema

Cada poema un pájaro que huye
del sitio señalado por la plaga.
Cada poema un traje de la muerte
por las calles y plazas inundadas
en la cera letal de los vencidos.
Cada poema un paso hacia la muerte,
una falsa moneda de rescate,
un tiro al blanco en medio de la noche
horadando los puentes sobre el río,
cuyas dormidas aguas viajan
de la vieja ciudad hacia los campos,
donde el día prepara sus hogueras.
Cada poema un tacto yerto
del que yace en la losa de las clínicas,
un ávido anzuelo que recorre
el limo blando de las sepulturas.
Cada poema un lento naufragio del deseo,
un crujir de los mástiles y jarcias
que sostienen el peso de la vida.
Cada poema un estruendo de lienzos que derrumban
sobre el rugir helado de las aguas
el albo aparejo del velamen.
Cada poema invadiendo y desgarrando
la amarga telaraña del hastío.
Cada poema nace de un ciego centinela
que grita al hondo hueco de la noche
el santo y seña de su desventura.
Agua de sueño, fuente de ceniza,
piedra porosa de los mataderos,
madera en sombra de las siemprevivas,
metal que dobla por los condenados,

Each Poem

Each poem a bird that flees
from the place marked by the scourge.
Each poem a grim reaper's costume
in streets and squares overflowing
with the fatal wax of the defeated.
Each poem a step toward death,
a ransom in counterfeit coin,
a shot at the target in the middle of the night,
punching through the bridges over the river
whose sleeping waters journey
from the old city to the fields
where day prepares its pyres.
Each poem the rigid touch
of one who lies on a hospital slab,
an eager fishhook trawling
the soft mud of tombs.
Each poem a slow shipwreck of desire,
a creaking of the masts and the rigging
that bear the weight of life.
Each poem a tumult of canvas
over the water's icy roar
as the snow-white apparel of the sail collapses.
Each poem invading and tearing
the bitter web of tedium.
Each poem is born of a blind sentry
who shouts the password of his ill fortune
into the night's deep cavity.
Dream water, spring of ashes,
porous slaughterhouse stone,
shaded wood of sempervivum,
metal ringing for the condemned,

aceite funeral de doble filo,
cotidiano sudario del poeta,
cada poema esparce sobre el mundo
al agrio cereal de la agonía.

funeral oil for the double-edged blade,
poet's daily shroud,
each poem scatters over the world
the bitter grain of anguish.

[C.A.]

Sonata

Otra vez el tiempo te ha traído
al cerco de mis sueños funerales.
Tu piel, cierta humedad salina,
tus ojos asombrados de otros días,
con tu voz han venido, con tu pelo.
El tiempo, muchacha, que trabaja
como loba que entierra a sus cachorros
como óxido en las armas de caza,
como alga en la quilla del navío,
como lengua que lame la sal de los dormidos,
como el aire que sube de las minas,
como tren en la noche de los páramos.
De su opaco trabajo nos nutrimos
como pan de cristiano o rancia carne
que se enjuta en la fiebre de los ghettos.
A la sombra del tiempo, amiga mía,
un agua mansa de acequia me devuelve
lo que guardo de ti para ayudarme
a llegar hasta el fin de cada día.

Sonata

Time has brought you once again
to the circle of my funereal dreams.
Your skin, a certain salty moisture,
and your eyes amazed by other days,
have come along with your voice, your hair.
Time, girl, time that labors
like a she-wolf burying its pups,
like rust on hunting guns,
like seaweed on a ship's keel,
like a tongue licking salt from sleeping bodies,
like air rising out of mine shafts,
like a train in the upland night.
We feed on its opaque labor
as on Christian bread or aged meat
cured in the fever of the ghettos.
In the shadow of time, my friend,
still waters of a channel reflect
what I have kept of you to help me
through to each day's end.

[C.A.]

Exilio

Voz del exilio, voz de pozo cegado,
voz huérfana, gran voz que se levanta
como hierba furiosa o pezuña de bestia,
voz sorda del exilio,
hoy ha brotado como una espesa sangre
reclamando mansamente su lugar
en algún sitio del mundo.
Hoy ha llamado en mí
el griterío de las aves que pasan en verde algarabía
sobre los cafetales, sobre las ceremoniosas hojas del
    banano,
sobre las heladas espumas que bajan de los páramos,
golpeando y sonando
y arrastrando consigo la pulpa del café
y las densas flores de los cámbulos.

Hoy, algo se ha detenido dentro de mí,
un espeso remanso hace girar,
de pronto, lenta, dulcemente,
rescatados en la superficie agitada de sus aguas,
ciertos días, ciertas horas del pasado,
a los que se aferra furiosamente
la materia más secreta y eficaz de mi vida.
Flotan ahora como troncos de tierno balso,
en serena evidencia de fieles testigos
y a ellos me acojo en este largo presente de exilado.
En el café, en casa de amigos, tornan con dolor desteñido
Teruel, Jarama, Madrid, Irún, Somosierra, Valencia
y luego Perpignan, Argelés, Dakar, Marsella.
A su rabia me uno, a su miseria
y olvido así quién soy, de dónde vengo,

Exile

Voice of exile, voice of a dried-up well,
orphan voice, vast voice that arises
like tenacious grass or the hoof of an animal,
the deaf voice of exile,
today it has welled up like a thick blood
meekly claiming a rightful place
in some part of the world.
Today it has called up in me
the screech of passing birds in a green tumult
over the growing coffee, the stately banana leaves,
over the icy spray that descends from the plains,
beating and sounding
and carrying with it the pulped flesh of coffee
and the thick flowers of the cambulos.

Today, something has taken root in me.
Suddenly, a heavy torpor sets in motion,
sweetly, slowly,
certain days, certain hours from the past,
saved on the ruffled surface of its waters,
to which are fiercely fastened
the most secret and vital matter of my life.
They float now like logs of the lightest balsa,
serene evidence of faithful witnesses,
and I welcome them in to the long present of exile.
In cafés, in the houses of friends,
they come back, in a kind of faded sorrow,
Teruel, Jarama, Madrid, Irún, Somosierra, Valencia,
and later, Perpignan, Algiers, Dakar, Marseilles.
I am one with their rage, their misery,
and so I forget who I am and where I come from,

hasta cuando una noche
comienza el golpeteo de la lluvia
y corre el agua por las calles en silencio
y un olor húmedo y cierto
me regresa a las grandes noches del Tolima
en donde un vasto desorden de aguas
grita hasta el alba su vocerío vegetal;
su destronado poder, entre las ramas del sombrío,
chorrea aún en la mañana
acallando el borboteo espeso de la miel
en los pulidos calderos de cobre.

Y es entonces cuando peso mi exilio
y mido la irrescatable soledad de lo perdido
por lo que de anticipada muerte me corresponde
en cada hora, en cada día de ausencia
que lleno con asuntos y con seres
cuya extranjera condición me empuja
hacia la cal definitiva
de un sueño que roerá sus propias vestiduras,
hechas de una corteza de materias
desterradas por los años y el olvido.

until, one night, when the rain begins to beat
and water runs in silence through the streets
and a damp, insistent smell
takes me back to the vast nights in Tolima
when a great turbulence of water
keeps up a vegetal rumble until dawn:
its unleashed power, among the branches of darkness,
is still dripping at morning,
hushing the thickening bubbles in the honey
in the polished vats of copper.

It is then that exile weighs on me
and I sense the unreachable loneliness of all things lost
against what remains till anticipated death
in every hour, in every day of absence
which I fill with business and with other beings
whose alien condition pushes me
toward the definitive quicklime
of a dream that gnaws away at its own clothing
formed of a crust of many matters
exiled by time and the fogs of forgetting.

[A.R.]

Sonata

Por los árboles quemados después de la tormenta.
Por las lodosas aguas del delta.
Por lo que hay de persistente en cada día.
Por el alba de las oraciones.
Por lo que tienen ciertas hojas
en sus venas color de agua
profunda y en sombra.
Por el recuerdo de esa breve felicidad
ya olvidada
y que fuera alimento de tantos años sin nombre.
Por tu voz de ronca madreperla.
Por tus noches por las que pasa la vida
en un galope de sangre y sueño.
Por lo que eres ahora para mí.
Por lo que serás en el desorden de la muerte.
Por eso te guardo a mi lado
como la sombra de una ilusoria esperanza.

Sonata

For the trees burnt out in the wake of the storm.
For the muddy waters of the delta.
For all that persists in every day.
For the prayers that rise at dawn.
For what certain leaves bear in their veins,
shadowy, the color of deep water.
For the memory of that brief happiness, now forgotten,
nourishment for so many nameless years.
For your voice, husky, mother of pearl.
For your nights through which life passes
in a gallop of blood and dreams.
For what you are now to me.
For what you will be to me in the muddle of death.
For all that, I keep you at my side
like the shadow of an illusory hope.

[A.R.]

Canción del este

A la vuelta de la esquina
un ángel invisible espera;
una vaga niebla, un espectro desvaído
te dirá algunas palabras del pasado.
Como agua de acequia, el tiempo
cava en ti su manso trabajo
de días y semanas,
de años sin nombre ni recuerdo.
A la vuelta de la esquina
te seguirá esperando vanamente
ese que no fuiste, ese que murió
de tanto ser tú mismo lo que eres.
Ni la más leve sospecha,
ni la más leve sombra
te indica lo que pudiera haber sido
ese encuentro. Y, sin embargo,
allí estaba la clave
de tu breve dicha sobre la tierra.

Song of the East

Around the corner
an invisible angel is waiting;
a vague mist, a faded specter
will address you with a few words from the past.
Within you, time, like channel water,
pursues its gentle, hollowing work
of days and weeks
of nameless, unremembered years.
Around the corner,
the one you were not, the one who died
of your being so much what you are,
will continue to wait in vain.
Not the faintest hunch
or the faintest shadow
to intimate what that encounter
might have meant. And yet
there lay the key
to your brief happiness on earth.

[C.A.]

Sonata

¿Sabes qué te esperaba tras esos pasos del arpa llamándote
de otro tiempo, de otros días?

¿Sabes por qué un rostro, un gesto, vistos desde el tren que
se detiene al final del viaje,

antes de perderte en la ciudad que resbala entre la niebla y
la lluvia, vuelven un día a visitarte, a decirte con unos
labios sin voz, la palabra que tal vez iba a salvarte?

¡A dónde has ido a plantar tus tiendas! ¡Por qué esa ancla
que revuelve las profundidades ciegamente y tú nada
sabes?

Una gran extensión de agua suavemente se mece en vastas
regiones ofrecidas al sol de la tarde;

aguas del gran río que luchan contra un mar en extremo
cruel y helado, que levanta sus olas contra el cielo y va
a perderlas tristemente en la lodosa sabana del delta.

Tal vez eso pueda ser.

Tal vez allí te digan algo.

O callen fieramente y nada sepas.

¿Recuerdas cuando bajó al comedor para desayunar y la
viste de pronto, más niña, más lejana, más bella que
nunca?

También allí esperaba algo emboscado.

Lo supiste por cierto sordo dolor que cierra el pecho.

Pero alguien habló.

Un sirviente dejó caer un plato.

Una risa en la mesa vecina,

algo rompió la cuerda que te sacaba del profundo pozo
como a José los mercaderes.

Hablaste entonces y sólo te quedó esa tristeza que ya sabes
y el dulceamargo encanto por su asombro ante el mundo,
alzado al aire

Sonata

Do you know what awaited you behind those harp notes,
  calling from another time, from other days?
Do you know why a face, an expression, glimpsed from
  the train as it pulled up at the end of the journey,
before you were swallowed by the city that drifts between
  fog and rain, comes back to visit you one day, with
  voiceless lips to speak the word that might have been
  about to save you?
What a place to pitch your tents! Why this anchor blindly
  stirring up the depths, and you so unawares?
A great expanse of water gently swaying in vast regions
  offered up to the afternoon sun;
waters of the great river battling an utterly cruel and
  cold sea, which flings its waves at the sky before
  letting them sadly lapse away in the delta's muddy
  savanna.
It may be possible.
It may be they will tell you something there.
Or remain fiercely silent, and you none the wiser.
Do you remember when she came down to the dining
  room for breakfast and you saw her suddenly, more
  girl-like, more remote, more beautiful than ever?
There too something lay in ambush.
You could tell by a certain dull pain clutching at your chest.
But somebody spoke.
A server dropped a plate.
Laughter at the next table,
something broke the rope that was hauling you out of the
  deep well as the merchantmen drew and lifted up
  Joseph.
Then you spoke and were left with nothing but the

de cada día como un estandarte que señalara tu presencia y
   el sitio de tus batallas.
¿Quién eres, entonces? ¿De dónde salen de pronto esos
   asuntos en un puerto y ese tema que teje la viola
tratando de llevarte a cierta plaza, a un silencioso y viejo
   parque con su estanque en donde navegan gozosos los
   veleros del verano?
No se puede saber todo.
No todo es tuyo.
No esta vez, por lo menos. Pero ya vas aprendiendo a
   resignarte y a dejar que
otro poco tuyo se vaya al fondo definitivamente
y quedes más solo aún y más extraño,
como un camarero al que gritan en el desorden matinal de
   los hoteles,
órdenes, insultos y vagas promesas, en todas las lenguas de
   la tierra.

familiar sadness and the bittersweet charm of her
wonder at the world, hoisted into the air
of every day like a standard to signal your presence and
the site of your battles.
Who are you, then? Where have they suddenly sprung
from, these matters to attend to in a port, and this
theme woven by a viola
trying to lead you to a certain square, to a quiet, old park,
in whose pond the summer sailboats glide with delight?
Not everything can be known.
Not everything is yours.
Not this time, anyway. But already you are learning to
resign yourself and let
another little piece of what is yours sink forever to the
bottom,
leaving you even more alone, more of a stranger,
like a waiter in the midst of a hotel's morning commotion,
target of orders, insults, and vague promises shouted in all
the tongues of the earth.

[C.A.]

Pregón de los hospitales

¡Miren ustedes cómo es de admirar la situación privilegiada de esta gran casa de enfermos!

¡Observen el dombo de los altos árboles cuyas oscuras hojas, siempre húmedas, protegidas por un halo de plateada pelusa, dan sombra a las avenidas por donde se pasean los dolientes!

¡Escuchen el amortiguado paso de los ruidos lejanos, que dicen de la presencia de un mundo que viaja ordenadamente al desastre de los años,

al olvido, al asombro desnudo del tiempo!

¡Abran bien los ojos y miren cómo la pulida uña del síntoma marca a cada uno con su signo de especial desesperanza!;

sin herirlo casi, sin perturbarlo, sin moverlo de su doméstica órbita de recuerdos y penas y seres queridos,

para él tan lejanos ya y tan extranjeros en su territorio de duelo.

¡Entren todos a vestir el *ojoso* manto de la fiebre y conocer el temblor seráfico de la anemia

o la transparencia cerosa del cáncer que guarda su materia muchas noches,

hasta desparramarse en la blanca mesa iluminada por un alto sol voltaico que zumba dulcemente!

¡Adelante señores!

Aquí terminan los deseos imposibles:

el amor por la hermana,

los senos de la monja,

los juegos en los sótanos,

la soledad de las construcciones,

las piernas de las comulgantes,

todo termina aquí, señores.

¡Entren, entren!

Proclamation of the Hospitals

See how superbly located it is, this great house of the ill!

Note the domes of the tall trees whose dark, perpetually moist leaves, protected by halos of silvery fuzz, shade the avenues where the bereaved walk up and down.

Listen to the muffled tread of distant noises, confirming the presence of a world on its orderly way toward the ruination of the years,

toward oblivion and the bare wonder of time!

Open your eyes, look and see how the symptom's polished fingernail marks each patient with the sign of a particular despair!

almost without inflicting a wound, without disturbing or displacing the invalid from the domestic sphere of memories and sorrows and loved ones,

so remote now, so foreign in their territory of mourning.

Come in, one and all, to don the holey cloak of fever and know anemia's seraphic shivering

or the waxy translucency of cancer, which hoards its material night after night

before spilling it on the white table lit by a high voltaic sun, sweetly humming away!

Step right in, gentlemen!

This is where impossible desires come to an end:

the love of one's sister,

the nun's breasts,

the games in the cellar,

the solitude of building blocks,

the legs of the women taking communion,

it all comes to an end here, gentlemen.

Come in, come in!

Obedientes a la pestilencia que consuela y da olvido, que purifica y concede la gracia.

¡Adelante!

Prueben

la manzana podrida del cloroformo,

el blando paso del éter,

la montera niquelada que ciñe la faz de los moribundos,

la ola granulada de los febrífugos,

la engañosa delicia vegetal de los jarabes,

la sólida lanceta que libera el último coágulo, negro ya y poblado por los primeros signos de la transformación.

¡Admiren la terraza donde ventilan algunos sus males como banderas en rehén!

¡Vengan todos

feligreses de las más altas dolencias!

¡Vengan a hacer el noviciado de la muerte, tan útil a muchos, tan sabio en dones que infestan la tierra y la preparan!

Submit to the pestilence that consoles and dispenses oblivion, that purifies and grants reprieve.

Step right in!

Try

the apple rotten with chloroform,

the soft tread of ether,

the nickel-plated cap that clings to the faces of the dying,

the granular surge of febrifuges,

the deceptive herbal delight of syrups,

the sturdy lancet dislodging the last clot, already black and harboring the first signs of transformation.

Admire the terrace where certain patients air their ills

like flags held hostage!

Come one and all,

parishioners of the highest infirmities!

Come, enter death's novitiate, so useful to many, so judicious with its gifts, which plague the earth and make it ready!

[C.A.]

El mapa

Solía referirse El Gaviero a su Mapa de los Hospitales de Ultramar y alguna vez llegó hasta mostrarlo a sus amigos, sin dar mayores explicaciones, es cierto, sobre el significado de algunas escenas que ilustraban la carta. Eran nueve en total y representaban lo que sigue:

I

Un jinete encarnado
galopa por la estepa.
Su sable alcanza al
sol atónito
que lo espera extendido
en un golfo bañado
de tibio silencio.

2

Las armas enterradas
en lo más espeso
del bosque
indican el nacimiento de un gran río.
Un guerrero herido señala
con énfasis el lugar.
Su mano llega hasta
el desierto
y sus pies descansan
en una hermosa ciudad
de plazas soleadas y blancas.

The Map

El Gaviero would often refer to his Map of the Overseas Hospitals, and once he went as far as to show it to his friends, without, it is true, giving any serious explanation of the meaning of certain scenes shown on the Map, nine in all, pictured as follows:

1

A scarlet horseman
gallops across the steppes.
His sabre reaches to
the baffled sun,
which waits for him, spread over
a bay bathed in
a tepid silence.

2

Weapons buried in
the thickest part
of the forest
mark the source of a great river.
A wounded warrior
points out the spot, insistently.
His hand stretches to
the desert
and his feet are resting on
an elegant city
with white, sunlit squares.

3

El Gran Jefe ofrece
la Pipa de la Paz
a un cazador de búfalos
cuya mirada cae distraída sobre
las tiendas de colores
y el humo acre de las hogueras.
Un ciervo se acerca tristemente.

4

Los frutos de un ingrato
sabor metálico, señalan
las Islas Lastimeras.
Un barco naufraga tranquilo
y los marinos reman hacia
la playa en donde un jabalí
entierra su presa. La arena
enceguese a los dioses.

5

Un aire frío pasa
sobre la dura concha
de los crustáceos.
Un gran alarido raya
el cielo con su helado
relámpago de ira.
Como un tapete gris
llegan la noche y el espanto.

3

The Great Chief offers
the pipe of peace
to a buffalo hunter
whose distracted gaze falls on
the colored tents
and the acrid smoke from the bonfires.
A crow flaps close on wings of woe.

4

Fruits with an unpleasant
metallic taste are signs of
the Doleful Islands.
A ship is gently sinking
and the sailors are pulling
for a beach where a wild boar
is burying its prey. The sand
is blinding to the gods.

5

Cold air passes over
the hard shells
of the crustaceans.
A great shriek splits
the sky with its frozen
lightning flash of rage.
Like a gray carpet, they
descend, night and terror.

6

La diligencia corre desbocada
y una mujer pide auxilio,
las ropas en desorden
y los cabellos al viento.
El conductor bebe un
gran vaso de sidra
reclinado con desgano
en un torso de mármol.
Los erizos señalan
la ruta con sus largas
espinas nocturnas.

7

Un hidroavión vuela
sobre la selva. Allá,
abajo, lo saludan las misioneras
que preparan el matrimonio
del cacique. Un olor a canela
se esparce por el ámbito
y va a confundirse con el
lejano zumbido de la nave.

8

Una ciudad cercada de alta piedra
esconde el rígido cadáver de la reina
y la carroña grave y dulce de su último
capricho, un vendedor de helados
peinado como una colegiala.

6

The runaway carriage bolts
and a woman screams for help,
her clothing in disorder,
her hair loose in the wind.
The driver downs a huge
flagon of cider,
leaning unconcerned against
a marble torso.
Hedgehogs mark the road
with their long
nocturnal spines.

7

A seaplane flies
over the jungle. There below
the missionaries wave
as they prepare for the wedding
of the chief. A whiff of cinnamon
spreads through the atmosphere
and on, to lose itself in
the fading drone of the plane.

8

A city walled in with vast stones
conceals the stiffened corpse of the queen
and the sweet, decaying flesh of her last
folly, an ice-cream seller,
his hair combed like a schoolgirl's.

9

Venus nace de la rala
copa de un cocotero
y en su diestra lleva
el fruto del banano
con la cáscara pendiente
como un tierno palio de oro.
Llega el Verano
y un pescador cambia
una libra de almejas
por una máscara de esgrima.

9

Venus emerges from the skimpy
crest of a coconut palm.
In her right hand she holds
the fruit of a banana
with the peeled skin hanging down
like a soft, golden canopy.
Summer arrives
and a fisherman exchanges
a pound of clams
for a fencing mask.

[A.R.]

Moirologhia

Un Cardo amargo se demora para siempre en tu garganta
    ¡oh Detenido!
Pesado cada uno de tus asuntos
no perteneces ya a lo que tu interés y vigilia reclamaban.
Ahora inauguras la fresca cal de tus nuevas vestiduras,
ahora estorbas, ¡oh Detenido!
Voy a enumerarte algunas de las especies de tu nuevo
    reino
desde donde no oyes a los tuyos deglutir tu muerte y
hacer memoria melosa de tus intemperancias.
Voy a decirte algunas de las cosas que cambiarán para ti,
¡oh yerto sin mirada!
Tus ojos te serán dos túneles de viento fétido, quieto,
    fácil, incoloro.
Tu boca moverá pausadamente la mueca de su
    desleimiento.
Tus brazos no conocerán más la tierra y reposarán en
    cruz,
vanos instrumentos solícitos a la carie acre que los
    invade.
¡Ay, desterrado! Aquí terminan todas tus sorpresas,
tus ruidosos asombros de idiota.
Tu voz se hará del callado rastreo de muchas y diminutas
    bestias de color pardo,
de suaves derrumbamientos de materia polvosa ya y
    elevada en pequeños túmulos
que remedan tu estatura y que sostiene el aire sigiloso y
    ácido de los sepulcros.

---

*Moirologhia es un lamento o treno que cantan las mujeres del Peloponeso
alrededor del féretro o la tumba del difunto.

Moirology

A harsh thistle is stuck forever in your throat, Oh Con-
    demned One!
Every one of your affairs has become a burden.
What your interests and concerns laid claim to are yours
    no more.
Now you try on the fresh lime of your new garments,
now you are an obstruction, Oh Condemned One!
I am going to go over for you some of the qualities of your
    new kingdom,
from whence you cannot hear your own ones swallowing
    down your death
and making a honeyed music of your excesses.
I am going to tell you some of the things that will change
    for you,
stiffened and sightless one!
Your eyes will be tunnels for the fetid wind, still, compli-
    ant, colorless.
Your mouth will slowly turn into the grimace of dissolution.
Your arms will never know again the earth and will be
    crossed in repose,
vain implements wary of the fetid rotting that invades
    them.
Oh Unearthed One! Here end all your surprises,
your voluble idiot's astonishments.
Your voice will carry discreet traces of many tiny dark-
    skinned creatures,
of quiet landslides of body-become-dust, now formed into
    little mounds

---

*Moirology is a lamentation or dirge that Peloponnesian women chant around
the bier or grave of the deceased.

Tus firmes creencias, tus vastos planes
para establecer una complicada fe de categorías y
    símbolos;
tu misericordia con otros, tu caridad en casa,
tu ansiedad por el prestigio de tu alma entre los vivos,
tus luces de entendido,
en qué negro hueco golpean ahora,
cómo tropiezan vanamente con tu materia en derrota.
De tus proezas de amante,
de tus secretos y nunca bien satisfechos deseos,
del torcido curso de tus apetitos,
qué decir, ¡oh sosegado!
De tu magro sexo encogido sólo mana ya la linfa rosácea
    de tus glándulas,
las primeras visitadas por el signo de la descomposición.
¡Ni una leve sombra quedará en la caja para testimoniar
    tus concupiscencias!
"Un día seré grande..." solías decir en el alba
de tu ascenso por las jerarquías.
Ahora lo eres, ¡oh Venturoso! y en qué forma.
Te extiendes cada vez más
y desbordas el sitio que te fuera fijado
en un comienzo para tus transformaciones.
Grande eres en olor y palidez,
en desordenadas materias que se desparraman y te
    prolongan.
Grande como nunca lo hubieras soñado,
grande hasta sólo quedar en tu lugar, como testimonio de
    tu descanso,
el breve cúmulo terroso de tus cosas más minerales y
    tercas.
Ahora, ¡oh tranquilo desheredado de las más gratas
    especies!,
eres como una barca varada en la copa de un árbol,

that rearrange your shape, that wear the sour and watchful
    air of sepulchers.
Your solid beliefs, your great schemes
to set up an intricate system of belief in symbols and
    categories;
your generosity to others, your gentleness at home,
your concern for your own good name among the living,
your flashes of understanding,
at what black hole are they knocking now,
as they clashed vainly with your dying substance.
Now, of your lover's prowess,
of your secret and never satisfied desires,
of the crooked current of your appetites,
what to say now, Oh Peaceful One!
Your meager, shriveled sex now yields up only the rosy
    distillation of your glands,
first to be touched by the signs of decomposition.
Not one faint shadow left in the box to testify to your
    concupiscence!
"One day I will be big..." you used to say in the dawn
of your rise through the hierarchies.
Now you are, Adventurous One, and in what form!
You spread out more and more
and you overflow the place that was dug for you
as a start for your further transformations.
Great you are in smell and pallor,
in miscellaneous matter that spills over and prolongs you.
Great as you have never dreamed,
great as to leave in your place, as witness to your rest,
the small and earthy mound of your most obstinate,
    mineral self.
Now, Gentle One, disinherited by the most graceful
    species!
you are like a barge stranded in the crest of a tree,

como la piel de una serpiente olvidada por su dueña en
  apartadas regiones,
como joya que guarda la ramera bajo su colchón astroso,
como ventana tapiada por la furia de las aves,
como música que clausura una feria de aldea,
como la incómoda sal en los dedos del oficiante,
como el ciego ojo de mármol que se enmohece y cubre de
  inmundicia,
como la piedra que da tumbos para siempre en el fondo de
  las aguas,
como trapos en una ventana a la salida de la ciudad,
como el piso de una triste jaula de aves enfermas,
como el ruido del agua en los lavatorios públicos,
como el golpe a un caballo ciego,
como el éter fétido que se demora sobre los techos,
como el lejano gemido del zorro
cuyas carnes desgarra una trampa escondida a la orilla del
  estanque,
como tanto tallo quebrado por los amantes en las tardes de
  verano,
como centinela sin órdenes ni armas,
como muerta medusa que muda su arco iris por la opaca
  leche de los muertos,
como abandonado animal de caravana,
como huella de mendigos que se hunden al vadear una
  charca que protege su refugio,
como todo eso ¡oh varado entre los sabios cirios!
¡Oh surto en las losas del ábside!

like the skin of a serpent forgotten by its mistress in
    far-off regions,
like a jewel kept by a harlot under her sordid mattress,
like a window stopped up by the fury of the birds,
like music that brings to a close a village fair,
like salt, awkward in the fingers of the official,
like the blind eye in the marble, moldered and covered
    with dirt,
like the stone that rolls over forever at the bottom of
    moving water,
like cloths hung in a window on the way out of the city,
like the bottom of a mournful cage of sick birds,
like the surge of water in public lavatories,
like a blow to a blind horse,
like the fetid atmosphere that lingers over the roofs,
like the far-off groan of the fox
whose flesh is torn by a trap hidden at the edge of the dam,
like so many grass-stalks crushed by lovers on summer
    afternoons,
like a sentry without orders, without arms,
like a dead medusa that replaces its rainbow with the
    opaque milk of the dead,
like an abandoned animal from the caravan,
like the tracks of beggars who drowned while fording a
    pond that protects their shelter
like everything that is, Oh You, grounded among the
    candles of wisdom,
anchored to the gravestones of the chapel!

[A.R.]

Soledad

En Mitad de la selva, en la más oscura noche de los grandes árboles, rodeado del húmedo silencio esparcido por las vastas hojas del banano silvestre, conoció El Gaviero el miedo de sus miserias más secretas, el pavor de un gran vacío que le acechaba tras sus años llenos de historias y de paisajes. Toda la noche permaneció El Gaviero en dolorosa vigilia, esperando, temiendo el derrumbe de su ser, su naufragio en las girantes aguas de la demencia. De estas amargas horas de insomnio le quedó al Gaviero una secreta herida de la que manaba en ocasiones la tenue linfa de un miedo secreto e innombrable. La algarabía de las cacatúas que cruzaban en bandadas la rosada extensión del alba, lo devolvió al mundo de sus semejantes y tornó a poner en sus manos las usuales herramientas del hombre. Ni el amor, ni la desdicha, ni la esperanza, ni la ira volvieron a ser los mismos para él después de su aterradora vigilia en la mojada y nocturna soledad de la selva.

Solitude

In the middle of the jungle, in the darkest night of the great trees, surrounded by a humid silence hovering over the huge leaves of the wild banana tree, the Gaviero came to know the fear of his most secret wretchedness, the terror of a great emptiness that had pursued him through years crowded with stories and landscapes. All night the Gaviero kept a dolorous watch, waiting, fearing the collapse of his being, its shipwreck in the eddying waters of dementia. These bitter hours of sleeplessness left the Gaviero with a hidden wound that on occasion oozed the faint lymph of a secret, unnamable fear. The clamor of flocks of cockatoos flying across the lengthening pink of dawn brought him back to the world of his fellow creatures and returned to his hands the usual devices of man. Love, misfortune, hope, rage were never again the same for him after his terrifying vigil in the damp nocturnal solitude of the jungle.

[E.G.]

Letanía

Esta era la letanía recitada por El Gaviero mientras se bañaba en las torrenteras del delta:

> Agonía de los oscuros
> recoge tus frutos.
> Miedo de los mayores
> disuelve la esperanza.
> Ansia de los débiles
> mitiga tus ramas.
> Agua de los muertos
> mide tu cauce.
> Campana de las minas
> modera tus voces.
> Orgullo del deseo
> olvida tus dones.
> Herencia de los fuertes
> rinde tus armas.
> Llanto de las olvidadas
> rescata tus frutos.

Y así seguía indefinidamente mientras el ruido de las aguas ahogaba su voz y la tarde refrescaba sus carnes laceradas por los oficios más variados y oscuros.

Litany

This is the litany pronounced by El Gaviero as he washed in the channels of the delta:

Agony of the Dark Ones
gathers your fruit.
Fear of the Great Ones
dissolves all hope.
Anguish of the Meek
soothes your branches.
Water of the Dead Ones
measures out your ditch.
Bells of the Mines
change your voices.
Pride of Desire
forgets your gifts.
Heritage of the Strong
subdues your arms.
Weeping of Forgotten Women
recovers your fruits.

And so he went on, while the sound of the water drowned out his voice, and the afternoon soothed its lacerated flesh in its many and varied rituals.

[A.R.]

Caravansary

Para Octavio y Marie-Jo

1

Están mascando hojas de betel y escupen en el suelo con la monótona regularidad de una función orgánica. Manchas de un líquido ocre se van haciendo alrededor de los pies nervudos, recios como raíces que han resistido el monzón. Todas las estrellas, allá arriba, en la clara noche bengalí, trazan su lenta trayectoria inmutable. El tiempo es como una suave materia detenida en medio del diálogo. Se habla de navegaciones, de azares en los puertos clandestinos, de cargamentos preciosos, de muertes infames y de grandes hambrunas. Lo de siempre. En el dialecto del Distrito de Birbhum, al oeste de Bengala, se ventilan los modestos negocios de los hombres, un sórdido rosario de astucias, mezquinas ambiciones, cansada lujuria, miedos milenarios. Lo de siempre, frente al mar en silencio, manso como una leche vegetal, bajo las estrellas incontables. Las manchas de betel en el piso de tierra lustrosa de grasas y materias inmemoriales van desapareciendo en la anónima huella de los hombres. Navegantes, comerciantes a sus horas, sanguinarios, soñadores y tranquilos.

2

Si te empeñas en dar crédito a las mentiras del camellero, a las truculentas historias que corren por los patios de las posadas, a las promesas de las mujeres cubiertas de velos y procaces en sus ofertas; si persistes en ignorar ciertas leyes nunca escritas sobre la conducta sigilosa que debe seguirse al cruzar tierras de infieles, si continúas en tu necedad, nunca

Caravansary

For Octavio and Marie-Jo

I

They chew betel leaves and spit on the ground with the monotonous regularity of a biological function. Around their sinewy feet, tough like roots that have held on through the monsoon, gobs of an ochre fluid multiply. All the stars overhead, in the clear Bengali night, trace their slow and changeless courses. Time is like a smooth material suspended in the midst of the conversation. The talk is of sea voyages, the vagaries of shadow ports, precious cargo, shameful deaths, great famines. Same old story. In the dialect of the Birbhum district in western Bengal, the humble affairs of mankind are aired, a sordid litany of tricks, petty ambitions, wearied lust, thousand-year-old fears. Same old story, facing the quiet sea, still as milky sap, beneath the innumerable stars. On the earthen floor that shines with grease and immemorial deposits, the betel gobs are vanishing into humanity's anonymous footprint. Sailors, occasional traders: cruel, fanciful, and calm.

2

If you will believe the camel driver's lies, the gruesome stories that circulate in the yards of inns, the promises of women covered in veils and lewd in their proposals; if you persist in ignoring certain never-written laws concerning the secretive conduct that must be observed when crossing the lands of the infidel; if you persevere in your folly, it will never be given to you to pass through the gates of the city

te será dado entrar por las puertas de la ciudad de Tashkent, la ciudad donde reina la abundancia y predominan los hombres sabios y diligentes. Si te empeñas en tu necedad...

3

¡Alto los enfebrecidos y alterados que con voces chillonas demandan lo que no se les debe! ¡Alto los necios! Terminó la hora de las disputas entre rijosos, ajenos al orden de estas salas. Toca ahora el turno a las mujeres, las egipcias reinas de Bohemia y de Hungría, las trajinadoras de todos los caminos; de sus ojos saltones, de sus altas caderas, destilará el olvido sus mejores alcoholes, sus más eficaces territorios. Afinquemos nuestras leyes, digamos nuestro canto y, por última vez, engañemos la especiosa llamada de la vieja urdidora de batallas, nuestra hermana y señora erguida ya delante de nuestra tumba. Silencio, pues, y que vengan las hembras de la pusta, las damas de Moravia, las egipcias a sueldo de los condenados.

4

Soy capitán del 3º de Lanceros de la Guardia Imperial, al mando del coronel Tadeuz Lonczynski. Voy a morir a consecuencia de las heridas que recibí en una emboscada de los desertores del Cuerpo de Zapadores de Hesse. Chapoteo en mi propia sangre cada vez que trato de volverme buscando el imposible alivio al dolor de mis huesos destrozados por la metralla. Antes de que el vidrio azul de la agonía invada mis arterias y confunda mis palabras, quiero confesar aquí mi amor, mi desordenado, secreto, inmenso, delicioso, ebrio amor por la condesa Krystina Krasinska, mi hermana. Que

of Tashkent, the city where abundance reigns and wise and diligent men hold sway. If you persist in your folly...

3

Enough of the feverish and agitated claimants, shrilly demanding what is not their due! Enough of fools! The time for bickering among the quarrelsome, mindless of the order of these courts, is past. Time now for the women, the Egyptian queens of Bohemia and Hungary, weariless on all the ways; from their bulging eyes, from their high hips, oblivion will distill its finest liquors, its most effective realms. Let us lay down our laws, intone our song, and for the last time let us elude the specious call of that old battle-plotter, our sister and mistress, already standing tall before our tomb. Silence, then, and let them come, the women of the puszta, the ladies of Moravia, the Egyptians in the pay of the condemned.

4

I am a captain in the Third Lancers Regiment of the Imperial Guard, under the command of Colonel Tadeuz Lonczynski. I shall die as a result of wounds inflicted during an ambush by deserters from the Corps of Sappers and Miners of Hesse. Each time I try to turn over, vainly attempting to ease the pain of my bones shattered by machine-gun fire, I splash in my own blood. Before the blue glass of the final agony infiltrates my arteries and scrambles my words, here I wish to confess my love, my unruly, secret, immense, delicious, drunken love for Countess Krystina Krasinska, my sister. May God forgive the grueling vigils of feverish desire for her that I endured in our last summer together at the family's

Dios me perdone las arduas vigilias de fiebre y deseo que pasé por ella, durante nuestro último verano en la casa de campo de nuestros padres en Katowicze. En todo instante he sabido guardar silencio. Ojalá se me tenga en cuenta en breve, cuando comparezca ante la Presencia Ineluctable. ¡Y pensar que ella rezará por mi alma al lado de su esposo y de sus hijos!

5

Mi labor consiste en limpiar cuidadosamente las lámparas de hojalata con las cuales los señores del lugar salen de noche a cazar el zorro en los cafetales. Lo deslumbran al enfrentarle súbitamente estos complejos artefactos, hediondos a petróleo y a hollín, que se oscurecen en seguida por obra de la llama que, en un instante, enceguece los amarillos ojos de la bestia. Nunca he oído quejarse a estos animales. Mueren siempre presas del atónito espanto que les causa esta luz inesperada y gratuita. Miran por última vez a sus verdugos como quien se encuentra con los dioses al doblar una esquina. Mi tarea, mi destino, es mantener siempre brillantes y listo este grotesco latón para su nocturna y breve función venatoria. ¡Y yo que soñaba ser algún día laborioso viajero por tierras de fiebre y aventura!

6

Cada vez que sale el rey de copas hay que tornar a los hornos, para alimentarlos con el bagazo que mantiene constante el calor de las pailas. Cada vez que sale el as de oros, la miel comienza a danzar a borbotones y a despedir un aroma inconfundible que reúne, en su dulcísima materia, las más secretas

country house in Katowice. Not once have I let a word slip. That, I hope, will be counted in my favor when shortly I appear before the Ineluctable Presence. And to think that she will pray for my soul beside her husband and her children!

5

My work consists of carefully cleaning the tin lamps used by the masters of this place when they go out at night to hunt foxes in the coffee plantations. They dazzle their prey by suddenly confronting it with these complex artifacts, which stink of soot and kerosene, and are soon darkened by the action of the flame, whose brightness, in an instant, blinds the creature's yellow eyes. I have never heard those animals whimper. They always die in the grip of the astonished horror provoked by that sudden light from nowhere. They gaze their last at the executioners like someone who has turned a corner and come face to face with the gods. My task, my destiny, is to keep these grotesque cans perpetually shiny and ready to serve their brief, nocturnal, venatic purpose. I who dreamed that someday I would be a tireless traveler in the lands of fever and adventure!

6

Whenever the king of cups is played, it is time to return to the ovens, to stoke them with the bagasse that keeps the pans at a constant heat. Each time the ace of coins is played, the syrup begins its bubbling dance, giving off an unmistakable scent, whose subtle substance combines the jungle's most secret essences and the cool, calm vapor that rises from the channels. The syrup is ready! The miracle of its joyful

esencias del monte y el fresco y tranquilo vapor de las acequias. ¡La miel está lista! El milagro de su alegre presencia se anuncia con el as de espadas. Pero si es el as de bastos el que sale, entonces uno de los paileros ha de morir cubierto por la miel que lo consume, como un bronce líquido y voraz vertido en la blanda cera del espanto. En la madrugada de los cañaverales, se reparten las cartas en medio del alto canto de los grillos y el escándalo de las aguas que caen sobre la rueda que mueve el trapiche.

7

Cruzaba los precipicios de la cordillera gracias a un ingenioso juego de poleas y cuerdas que él mismo manejaba, avanzando lentamente sobre el abismo. Un día, las aves lo devoraron a medias y lo convirtieron en un pingajo sanguinolento que se balanceaba al impulso del viento helado de los páramos. Había robado una hembra de los constructores del ferrocarril. Gozó con ella una breve noche de inagotable deseo y huyó cuando ya le daban alcance los machos ofendidos. Se dice que la mujer lo había impregnado en una sustancia nacida de sus vísceras más secretas y cuyo aroma enloqueció a las grandes aves de las tierras altas. El despojo terminó por secarse al sol y tremolaba como una bandera de escarnio sobre el silencio de los precipicios.

8

En Akaba dejó la huella de su mano en la pared de los abrevaderos.

En Gdynia se lamentó por haber perdido sus papeles en una riña de taberna, pero no quiso dar su verdadero nombre.

presence is announced by the ace of swords. But if the ace of batons is played, one of the men who tends the pans must die, covered in syrup that eats him away, like voracious, liquid bronze poured onto the soft wax of horror. At dawn in the cane fields, the cards are dealt to the shrill song of the crickets and the racket of water falling on the wheel that powers the sugar mill.

7

He used to cross the chasms of the cordillera by means of an ingenious system of pulleys and ropes that he could operate on his own, slowly advancing over the abyss. One day, he was half devoured by birds, leaving a bloody, tattered bundle to swing in the icy wind that blows from the uplands. He had stolen a woman from the railway builders. With her he enjoyed a brief night of inexhaustible desire, and when the affronted men were about to lay hands on him, he fled. They say that the woman had impregnated him with a substance secreted in her innermost recesses, whose scent drove the great raptors of the high country mad. His remains eventually dried out in the sun and fluttered like a flag of derision over the silence of the chasms.

8

In Aqaba he left the print of his hand on the rock wall by the springs.

In Gdynia he regretted having lost his papers in a tavern brawl but refused to give his real name.

In Recife he offered the bishop his services and ended up stealing a tin monstrance coated with pinchbeck.

En Recife ofreció sus servicios al Obispo y terminó robándose una custodia de hojalata con un baño de similor.

En Abidján curó la lepra tocando a los enfermos con un cetro de utilería y recitando en tagalo una página del memorial de aduanas.

En Valparaíso desapareció para siempre, pero las mujeres del barrio alto guardan una fotografía suya en donde aparece vestido como un agente viajero. Aseguran que la imagen alivia los cólicos menstruales y preserva a los recién nacidos contra el mal de ojo.

9

Ninguno de nuestros sueños, ni la más tenebrosa de nuestras pesadillas, es superior a la suma total de fracasos que componen nuestro destino. Siempre iremos más lejos que nuestra más secreta esperanza, sólo que en sentido inverso, siguiendo la senda de los que cantan sobre las cataratas, de los que miden su propio engaño con la sabia medida del uso y del olvido.

10

Hay un oficio que debiera prepararnos para las más sordas batallas, para los más sutiles desengaños. Pero es un oficio de mujeres y les será vedado siempre a los hombres. Consiste en lavar las estatuas de quienes amaron sin medida ni remedio y dejar enterrada a sus pies una ofrenda que, con el tiempo, habrá carcomido los mármoles y oxidado los más recios metales. Pero sucede que también este oficio desapareció hace ya tanto tiempo, que nadie sabe a ciencia cierta cuál es el orden que debe seguirse en la ceremonia.

In Abidjan he cured lepers by touching them with a costume scepter and reciting a page from a customs brief in Tagalog.

In Valparaíso he disappeared forever, but the women of the upper district have kept a photograph in which he is dressed as a traveling salesman. They swear that the image relieves period pain and protects newborns against the evil eye.

9

Not one of our dreams, not even our most sinister nightmare, can surpass the sum total of failures that constitute our destiny. We will always go further than we had most secretly hoped but in the opposite direction, following the way of those who sing above the cataracts, who measure their illusions against the wise scale of custom and forgetting.

10

There is an occupation that should prepare us for the quietest battles, the subtlest disappointments. But it belongs to women and will always be forbidden to men. It consists of washing the statues of those who loved beyond measure, without hope, and leaving an offering buried at their feet, which over time will eat through marble and corrode the most resistant metals. But this occupation too, it turns out, disappeared so long ago that no one can be sure of the order to be followed in the ceremony.

INVOCACIÓN

¿Quién convocó aquí a estos personajes?
¿Con qué voz y palabras fueron citados?
¿Por qué se han permitido usar
el tiempo y la sustancia de mi vida?
¿De dónde son y hacia dónde los orienta
el anónimo destino que los trae a desfilar frente a nosotros?

Que los acoja, Señor, el olvido.
Que en él encuentren la paz,
el deshacerse de su breve materia,
el sosiego a sus almas impuras,
la quietud de sus cuitas impertinentes.

No sé, en verdad, quiénes son,
ni por qué acudieron a mí
para participar en el breve instante
de la página en blanco.
Vanas gentes estas,
dadas, además, a la mentira.
Su recuerdo, por fortuna,
comienza a esfumarse
en la piadosa nada
que a todos habrá de alojarnos.
Así sea.

INVOCATION

Who summoned these characters?
With what voice and words were they called?
Why have they presumed to use
the time and the substance of my life?
Where are they from, and where are they bound,
led by the nameless destiny that has brought them to
    parade before us?

Lord, may oblivion take them in.
Let them find peace there
and the coming apart of their transient matter,
and tranquillity for their impure souls,
and relief from their untimely tribulations.

Truly, I do not know who they are
nor why they came to me
to participate in the brief moment
of the still-blank page.
Hollow people these,
and prone, besides, to lying.
Luckily their memory
is beginning to fade
into the merciful nothingness
that will at length accommodate us all.
So be it.

[C.A.]

La nieve del amiral

Para J. G. Cobo Borda

Soy el desordenado hacedor de las más escondidas rutas, de los más secretos atracaderos. De su inutilidad y de su ignota ubicación se nutren mis días.

Guarda ese pulido guijarro. A la hora de tu muerte podrás acariciarlo en la palma de tu mano y ahuyentar así la presencia de tus más lamentables errores, cuya suma borra de todo posible sentido tu vana existencia.

Todo fruto es un ojo ciego ajeno a sus más suaves substancias.

Hay regiones en donde el hombre cava en su felicidad las breves bóvedas de un descontento sin razón y sin sosiego.

Sigue a los navíos. Sigue las rutas que surcan las gastadas y tristes embarcaciones. No te detengas. Evita hasta el más humilde fondeadero. Remonta los ríos. Desciende por los ríos. Confúndete en las lluvias que inundan las sabanas. Niega toda orilla.

Noten cuánto descuido reina en estos lugares. Así los días de mi vida. No fue más. Ya no podrá serlo.

Las mujeres no mienten jamás. De los más secretos repliegues de su cuerpo mana siempre la verdad. Sucede que nos ha sido dado descifrarla con una parquedad implacable. Hay muchos que nunca lo consiguen y mueren en la ceguera sin salida de sus sentidos.

The Snow of the Admiral

For J. G. Cobo Borda

I am the disordered creator of the most obscure routes, the most secret moorings. Their uselessness, their undiscovered location are what feed my days.

Keep that polished pebble. At the hour of your death you can caress it in the palm of your hand and use it to drive away the presence of your lamentable errors which, taken together, erase all possible significance from your vain existence.

Every fruit is blind to its gentler substances. There are regions where man digs out of his happiness the small, underground chambers of a discontent without reason or cure.

Follow the ships. Follow the routes plowed by worn, melancholy vessels. Don't stop. Avoid even the humblest anchorage. Sail up the rivers, down the rivers. Lose yourself in the rains that flood the savannas. Deny all shores.

Take note of the neglect that reigns here. Like the days of my life. That's all it was. It will never be otherwise.

Women never lie. Truth always pours from the most secret folds of their bodies. Our lot is to interpret it with an implacable paucity. Many men never can and die in the inescapable blindness of their senses.

Two metals exist that prolong life and sometimes grant happiness. Not gold or silver or anything else you can imagine. I only know they exist.

Dos metales existen que alargan la vida y conceden, a veces, la felicidad. No son el oro, ni la plata, ni cosa que se les parezca. Solo sé que existen.

Hubiera yo seguido con las caravanas. Hubiera muerto enterrado por los camelleros, cubierto con la bosta de sus rebaños, bajo el alto cielo de las mesetas. Mejor, mucho mejor hubiera sido. El resto, en verdad, ha carecido de interés.

I should have followed the caravans. I would have died and been buried by the camel drivers and covered by the dung of their herds under the lofty tableland sky. It would have been better, much better. All the rest has truly lacked interest.

[E.G.]

Cocora

I stayed here to take care of the mine, and by now I've lost track of how many years I've been in this place. Undoubtedly a good many, because the path that led to the mine shafts and ran along the riverbank is overgrown with brush and plantains. Several guava trees are growing in the middle of the trail and have produced quite a few harvests. The owners and operators have probably forgotten all about it, and no wonder. They never found ore no matter how deep they dug or how many branches they made off the main tunnels. And I, a seaman for whom ports were mere pretexts for transient loves and brothel fights, who can still feel in my bones the sway of the crow's nest when I climbed to the top to watch the horizon and give storm warnings, to call out sightings of coastlines and pods of whales and dizzying schools of fish that ap-proached the ship like a drunken mob, here I am, visiting the cool darkness of these labyrinths where a wind that is often warm and damp carries voices, laments, the unending, relentless toil of insects, the fluttering wings of dark butterflies, the screech of a bird lost in the depths of the mine shafts.

I sleep in what they called the Ensign's Gallery, the driest of the shafts, whose entrance faces a cliff that drops sharply to the turbulent river. On rainy nights I can smell it flooding: a muddy, sharp scent of bruised plants and animals broken against the rocks; a smell of anemic blood like the odor of women worn out by the hard climate of the tropics—the smell of a world coming apart precedes the drunken savagery of water rising in immense, devastating wrath.

I would like to leave a record of some of the things I've seen during my long days of idleness, for familiarity with deep places has turned me into someone very different from

the man I used to be in the years I sailed oceans and rivers. Perhaps the acid breath of the galleries has altered or sharpened my ability to perceive the secret, intangible, yet rich life that inhabits these pits of misfortune. I'll begin with the principal gallery. One enters along an avenue of cámbulo trees whose hardy orange blossoms create a carpet that sometimes extends all the way down to the bottom. The deeper one penetrates the gallery the dimmer the light, though it shines with inexplicable intensity on the flowers blown far inside by the wind. I lived there for a long time and had to leave only because at the start of the rains I would hear voices, incomprehensible whispers like the prayers of women at a wake, yet the sounds of laughter and scuffling, which were in no way funereal, made me think of some obscene act prolonged endlessly in the hollow dark. I resolved to decipher what the voices were saying, and after listening for days and nights with feverish attention, I finally made out the word "Viana." At about the same time I fell ill, apparently with malaria, and could only lie on the straw pallet I used for a bed. For long periods I was delirious, and that lucidity, honed by fever beneath the superficial confusion of its symptoms, allowed me to begin a conversation with the women. Their honeyed attitude and obvious duplicity filled me with silent, humiliating fear. One night, obeying mysterious secret impulses made more intense by my delirium, I sat up and shouted words that echoed and re-echoed against the walls of the mine. "Shut up, you bitches! I was a friend to the Prince of Viana! Respect the highest misery, the crown of those beyond salvation!" A dense silence that continued after the echoes of my shouts had faded away washed me up on the shores of my fever. I waited all night, bathed in the sweat of returning health. The silence remained, drowning out even the sound of humble creatures at their labor of leaves and secretions that weave the intangible. A milky

light announced the dawn, I managed somehow to crawl out of that gallery, and I never went back again.

Another shaft is the one the miners called the Stag. It's not very deep, but through some quirk in the engineers' design an absolute darkness reigns there. Only by touch could I find my way around the gallery, which was filled with tools and carefully nailed boxes. These gave off an odor impossible to describe. It was like the smell of a gelatin made with the most secret distillations from some improbable metal. But what kept me in there for days on end, on the verge of losing my reason, was something standing at the very end of the gallery, leaning against the wall that marks the bottom of the shaft. Something that might be called a machine if it weren't for the impossibility of moving any of its apparent parts. Metal pieces of every shape and size, cylinders, spheres, all fixed in rigid immobility, made up the unspeakable structure. I could never find the end of it or measure the misbegotten thing, which was attached on all sides to the rock, its design of polished steel looming as if intending to be a definitive representation of nothingness in this world. One day, when my hands grew weary after weeks and weeks of feeling the complex connections, the rigid pinions, the frozen spheres, I ran away, horrified to find myself pleading with the indefinable presence to reveal its secret, the ultimate and true reason for its existence. I haven't gone back to that part of the mine either, but on certain hot, humid nights the silent metal presence visits my dreams, and the terror of it makes me sit up in bed with racing heart and trembling hands. No earthquake or landslide, however gigantic, can make this ineluctable mechanism in the service of eternity disappear.

The third shaft is the one I mentioned at the start, the one called the Ensign's Gallery. I'm living there now. A peaceful darkness extends to the deepest part of the tunnel,

and the river, crashing against the stone walls and great boulders at the foot of the cliff, lends a certain joy to the atmosphere—a break, however precarious, in the endless tedium of my job as caretaker of this abandoned mine.

It's true that every so often gold prospectors come this far upriver to wash sand in their wooden pans. The acrid smell of cheap tobacco lets me know they've arrived. I go down to watch them work, and we exchange a few words. They come from distant regions, and I barely understand their language. I'm astounded by their infinite patience in labor that demands so much attention to detail and gives such poor results. The women of the cane planters on the opposite bank also come here occasionally. They wash their clothes in the river and pound them against the rocks. That's how I know they're here. I've had relations with a few who climb up to the mine with me. Hurried, anonymous encounters, less a matter of pleasure than a need to feel another body against my skin and fend off, even with that brief touch, the solitude that is consuming me.

One day I'll leave, follow the riverbank until I find the road to the uplands, and then I hope forgetting can help erase the wretched time I've spent here.

[E.G.]

In the Marshes

Before penetrating the marshes, the time had come for the Gaviero to review the moments of his life from which there had flowed, with regular and gratifying constancy, the reason for his days, the sequence of motives that had always overcome the gentle call of death.

They were sailing down the river in a rusty barge that had once been used to carry fuel oil to the uplands and had been retired from service many years before. An asthmatic diesel engine struggled to push the vessel along to the catastrophic clang of metal against metal.

There were four travelers on the barge. They had been eating fruit, much of it still green, which they picked on the bank when they pulled ashore to repair another breakdown in the infernal machinery. At times they consumed the flesh of drowned animals that floated on the muddy surface of the water.

Two of the travelers died in silent convulsions after devouring a water rat that, as they killed it, stared at them with the fixed wrath of its bulging eyes like two demented, incandescent carbuncles confronting a painful, inexplicable death.

The Gaviero remained, accompanied by a woman who had been wounded in a brothel fight and came aboard at one of the ports in the interior. Her clothes were torn and her dark, unruly hair was flattened in places by dried blood. Her scent was bittersweet, fruity and feline. The woman's wounds healed easily, but an attack of malaria left her prostrate in a hammock that hung from the metal supports of the precarious tin roof protecting the tiller and controls. The Gaviero did not know if the sick woman's body trembled with attacks of fever or because of the vibrating propeller.

Maqroll sat on a plank bench and steered the barge in the middle of the river. He let the river carry them, not trying to avoid the whirlpools and sandbars, which became more frequent as they approached the marshes where the river began to merge with the sea, extending silently and effortlessly into a horizon of saline swamp.

One day the motor suddenly fell silent. The metal parts had been vanquished by the unrelenting struggle to which they had been subjected for so many years. A great quiet descended on the travelers. The bubbling water against the flat prow of the barge and the faint moaning of the sick woman lulled the Gaviero into tropical somnolence.

Then, in the lucid delirium of implacable hunger, he was able to isolate the most familiar, recurrent signs that had nourished the substance of certain times in his life. What follows are some of those moments, summoned by Maqroll the Gaviero as he drifted into the marshes at the river's mouth:

A coin that fell from his hands and rolled down a street in the port of Antwerp, until it was lost in a sewer drain.

The song of a girl hanging clothes on the deck of a freighter as it waited for the sluice gates to open.

The sun gilding the wooden bed where he slept with a woman whose language he could not understand.

The air in the trees announcing the coolness that would restore his strength when he reached La Arena.

His conversation with a peddler of miraculous medals in a tavern in Turko-Limanon.

The roar of the torrent in the ravine drowning out the voice of the woman in the coffee groves who always came to him when all hope was lost.

The fire, yes, the flames licking with implacable urgency at the high walls of a castle in Moravia.

The clink of glasses in a sordid bar on the Strand where he learned the other face of evil that dissolves, slowly and with no surprise, at the indifference of those present.

The feigned moaning of two old whores who, naked and entwined, imitated the ancient rite of desire in a dingy room in Istanbul whose windows overlooked the Bosphorus. The performers' eyes stared at the stained walls while the kohl ran down their ageless cheeks.

A long, imaginary dialogue with the Prince of Viana and the Gaviero's plans for an action in Provence designed to save an improbable inheritance of the unfortunate heir to the house of Aragón.

A certain sliding of the parts of a firearm when it has just been oiled after a meticulous cleaning.

The night when the train stopped at the burning ravine. The din of water smashing against the great rocks, almost invisible in the milky starlight. A cry in the banana groves. Solitude corroding like rust. The vegetal breath coming out of the darkness.

All the stories and lies about his past accumulating until they formed another being, always present and naturally

more deeply loved than his own pale, useless existence composed of nausea and dreams.

A crack of wood waking him in the humble hotel on the Rue du Rempart and, in the middle of the night, leaving him on that shore where only God is aware of other people.

The eyelid twitching with the autonomous speed of one who knows he is in the hands of death. The eyelid of the man he had to kill, with repugnance, with no anger, to save the life of a woman whom he now found unbearable.

All his waiting. All the emptiness of that nameless time used up in the foolishness of negotiations, proceedings, journeys, blank days, mistaken itineraries. All that life, from which he now begs, as he slips through the wounded dark toward death, some of the leftover scraps he thinks he has a right to.

Some days later a customs launch found the barge run aground among the mangroves. The woman, deformed by extraordinary swelling, gave off an unbearable stench that spread like the limitless swamp. The Gaviero lay curled up beside the tiller, his body dried and sere like a pile of roots withered by the sun. His wide-open eyes were fixed on that nothingness, immediate and anonymous, where the dead find the rest that was denied them during their wanderings when they were alive.

[E.G.]

Razón del extraviado

Para Alastair Reid

Vengo del norte,
donde forjan el hierro, trabajan las rejas,
hacen las cerraduras, los arados,
las armas incansables,
donde las grandes pieles de oso
cubren paredes y lechos,
donde la leche espera la señal de los astros,
del norte donde toda voz es una orden,
donde los trineos se detienen
bajo el cielo sin sombra de tormenta.
Voy hacia el este,
hacia los más tibios cauces
de la arcilla y el limo,
hacia el insomnio vegetal y paciente
que alimentan las lluvias sin medida;
hacia los esteros voy, hacia el delta
donde la luz descansa absorta
en las magnolias de la muerte
y el calor inaugura vastas regiones
donde los frutos se descomponen
en una densa siesta
mecida por los élitros
de insectos incansables.
Y, sin embargo, aún me inclinaría
por las tiendas de piel, la parca arena,
por el frío reptando entre las dunas
donde canta el cristal
su atónita agonía
que arrastra el viento
entre túmulos y signos
y desvía el rumbo de las caravanas.

The Wanderer's Tale

For Alastair Reid

I come from the North,
where they forge iron,
where they make locks and grills,
iron gates and inexhaustible arms,
where great bearskins cover walls and litters,
where the milk waits for a signal from the stars;
from the North, where every voice speaks an order,
where the sledges draw their breath under a sky
with no shadow of storm.
I am going eastward, toward the warmest channels
of mud and clay,
and the patient, vegetal sleeplessness
fed by the immeasurable waters.
It's to the estuaries I'm finally going,
to the delta where the light rests, brooding on
the magnolias of death,
and the heat spreads across vast regions
in a dense siesta
lulled by the wings
of restless insects.
Even so, I would still yearn for
the leather workshops, the sparse sand,
the cold slithering through the dunes
where the glass sings
and the wind scourges
the ground and the grave-mounds,
blurring the tracks of the caravans.
I came from the North.
Ice annulled the labyrinths
where the sword obeys
the summons to its destiny.

Vine del norte,
el hielo canceló los laberintos
donde el acero cumple
la señal de su aventura.
Hablo del viaje, no de sus etapas.
En el este la luna vela
sobre el clima que mis llagas
solicitan como alivio
de un espanto tenaz y sin remedio.

I speak of traveling, not of resting places.
In the East, the moon broods over the region
that my hurt self reaches out to for relief
from a clutching fear, a fear that has no cure.

[A.R.]

The Gaviero's Visit

For Gilberto Aceves Navarro

His appearance had changed completely. Not that he looked older, more worn by the passing years and the harsh climates he frequented. He hadn't been away that long. It was something else. Something revealed in his weary, oblique gaze. Something in his shoulders, which had lost all their expressive movement and were held rigid, as if they no longer had to bear the weight of life or the prodding of its joys and sorrows. His voice had become noticeably muted and had a velvety, neutral tone. It was the voice of a man who speaks because the silence of others would be unbearable.

He carried a rocking chair to the gallery that faced the coffee plantings on the riverbank and sat down with an expectant air, as if the night breeze that would not be long in coming might relieve his profound but indeterminate misfortune. The water crashing against the great rocks provided a distant accompaniment to his words and brought an opaque joy to the monotonous recounting of his affairs, which had not changed but were submerged now in an indifferent, toneless chant that betrayed his present condition of hopeless defeat. He was a hostage of the void.

"I sold women's clothing at the Guásimo ford where upland women crossed the river on fiesta days, and since they had to cross the river on foot and their clothes got wet even though they hiked them up above their waists, they would buy something from me so they wouldn't have to walk into town looking bedraggled.

"There was a time when that procession of dark, powerful thighs, round, firm buttocks, bellies like the breast of a dove, would have excited me to frenzy. I left the place when a jealous brother came after me with a machete because he thought I was making advances to a smiling green-eyed girl

when I was only measuring her for a skirt of flowered percale. She stopped him in time. A sudden disgust made me sell all my goods in a few hours and go away forever.

"That was when I lived for a few months in an abandoned railroad car on the tracks they never finished laying. I once told you about it. Besides, it's not important.

"After that I went down to the ports and signed on a freighter headed for fogbound, unmercifully cold places. To pass the time and relieve my boredom, I would go down to the machine room and tell the stokers the story of the last four Grand Dukes of Burgundy. I had to shout over the roaring boilers and clattering rods. They always asked me to repeat the death of John the Fearless at the hands of the king's men on Montereau Bridge, and the celebration of the marriage of Charles the Bold to Marguerite of York. Eventually that was all I did during our endless passage through fog and great blocks of ice. The captain forgot I existed until the chief petty officer went to him one day with the story that I wasn't letting the stokers do their work and was filling their heads with tales of bloody assassinations and outrageous attempts on the lives of great men. He'd heard me tell about the end of the last duke in Nancy, and who knows what the poor man thought. They put me ashore in a port along the Scheldt, my only possessions the patched rags on my back and an inventory of anonymous graves in the cemeteries on Mount Saint Lazarus.

"Then I dedicated myself to preaching and praying at the entrance to the Main River refineries. I announced the coming of a new Kingdom of God in which a strict, detailed interchange of sins and penitences would be established so that an inconceivable shock or a joy as brief as it was intense might be waiting for us at any hour of the day or night. I sold small sheets printed with litanies for a good death, in which the essentials of the doctrine were summarized. I've forgotten

most of them, although I sometimes remember three invocations in my dreams:

ingot of life, shed thy scales
wellspring of water, gather in the shadows
angel of mire, cut thy wings

"I often wonder whether these lines really formed part of the litany or if they are the offspring of my mournful, recurrent dreams. This isn't the time to find out, and it really doesn't interest me."

The Gaviero abruptly halted the tale of his increasingly precarious wanderings and launched into a long, rambling, apparently pointless monologue that I remember with painful fidelity and a vague revulsion I cannot account for.

"Because in the end all these trades, encounters, places, have stopped being the true substance of my life, to such an extent that I don't know which are products of my imagination and which belong to real experience. By means of them, through them, I try in vain to escape the obsessions that are certainly real, permanent, and true, and that weave the final chain of events, the evident destination of my journey through the world. It isn't easy to isolate them and give them a name, but they are roughly these:

"To settle for a happiness like that of certain childhood days in exchange for a shortened life.

"To prolong solitude and not fear the encounter with what we really are, with the man who talks to us and always hides so we won't sink into inescapable terror.

"To realize that nobody listens to anybody, nobody knows anything about anybody. That the word is mere deception, a trap that covers, disguises, buries the precarious structure

of our dreams and truths, all of them bearing the mark of the incommunicable.

"To learn, above all, to distrust memory. What we believe we remember is completely alien to, completely different from what really happened. So many moments of irritating, wearisome disgust are returned to us years later by memory as splendidly happy episodes. Nostalgia is the lie that speeds our approach to death. To live without remembering may be the secret of the gods.

"When I tell about my wanderings, my failures, my simple-minded deliriums and secret orgies, it is only to choke off, almost in midair, the animal screams, the piercing howls from the cave that would express more accurately what I really feel and what I really am. But I'm losing myself in digressions, and that isn't why I came."

His eyes took on a leaden stare, as if he were looking at a thick wall of colossal proportions. His lower lip trembled slightly. He folded his arms across his chest and began to rock slowly, as if trying to keep time to the sound of the river. A smell of fresh mud, of crushed vegetation and rotting sap, indicated that the waters were rising. The Gaviero was silent for a long time, until night fell with that dizzying explosion of darkness typical of the tropics. Intrepid fireflies danced in the warm silence of the coffee plantings. He began to speak, lost in another digression whose significance escaped me as he entered the darkest zones of his being. When he returned suddenly to events from his past, I could follow his monologue again.

"I've had few surprises in life," he said, "and none of them is worth the telling, but for me each has the mournful energy of a bell tolling catastrophe. One morning, in the stupefying heat of a river port, while I was putting on my clothes in a shabby room in a miserable brothel, I found a photograph of my father hanging on the wooden wall. He was sitting in a

wicker rocking chair on the verandah of a white hotel in the Caribbean. During her long widowhood my mother always kept that photograph in the same spot on her night table. 'Who's that?' I asked the woman I'd spent the night with; only now could I see all the wretched disorder of her flesh, the animality of her face. 'My father,' she answered with a sorrowful smile that revealed her toothless mouth, and she covered her fat nakedness with a sheet soaked in perspiration and misery. 'I never knew him, but my mother, she worked here too, she always remembered him and even kept some of his letters, like that could keep her young forever.' I finished dressing and went out to the wide, unpaved street that was blasted by sun, blaring radios, the clatter of cutlery and dishes in the cafés and cantinas beginning to fill with their regular clientele of truck drivers, cattle dealers, and soldiers from the air base. I thought with faint sadness that this was precisely the corner of life I would never have wanted to turn. Bad luck.

"Another time I went to a hospital in the Amazon after an attack of malaria that was draining my strength and keeping me delirious with fever. The heat at night was unbearable, yet it saved me from the whirlpools of vertigo whose center was some trivial phrase or the tone of a voice I couldn't identify, the fever spinning around it until all my bones ached. In the next bed a trader who'd been bitten by a gangrene spider was fanning the black pustule that covered his left side. 'This'll dry up soon, this'll dry up soon and I'll get out and close the deal. I'll be so rich I'll forget all about this hospital and the goddamn jungle that's only fit for monkeys and alligators.' The deal had something to do with a complicated traffic in spare parts for the seaplanes that flew the area with preferential import licenses, issued by the Army, which made them exempt from customs inspection and taxes. At least that's what I dimly remember, because all

night the man babbled about the smallest details of the affair, and one by one they became part of the whirling crises of my malaria. Finally, at dawn, I managed to fall asleep, but I was besieged by pain and panic that lasted all day and far into the night. 'Look, here are the papers. They'll get all screwed up. You'll see. Tomorrow I leave for sure,' he said one night, and repeated the words with fierce insistence as he brandished a handful of blue and pink papers covered with stamps and captions in three languages. The last thing I heard him say before I succumbed to a long bout of fever was: 'Oh, what a relief, what joy. This shit is over!' The thunder of a gunshot woke me. It sounded like the end of the world. I looked at my neighbor: his head, shattered by the bullet, was still quivering, as mushy as a rotten fruit. I was moved to another room, where I hung between life and death until the cool breezes of the rainy season brought me back to life.

"I don't know why I'm telling you this. I really came to leave these papers with you. You'll know what to do with them if we don't see each other again. They're letters from my youth, some pawn tickets, and a rough draft of the book I'll never finish. A study of the real reasons that Cesare Borgia, Duke of Valentinois, went to the court of his brother-in-law, the king of Navarre, and helped him in the struggle against the king of Aragón. How he died at dawn, ambushed by soldiers in the outskirts of Viana. There are twists behind this story, dark areas I once thought were worth clarifying. That was years ago. I'm also leaving an iron cross that I found in an Almogávar ossuary in the garden of an abandoned mosque in an Anatolian suburb. It's always brought me good luck, but I think the time has come to travel without it. And here are the bills and vouchers that prove my innocence in that matter of the explosives factory at the Sereno mines. The Hungarian medium who was my companion at the time,

and a Paraguayan partner and I—we were going to retire to Madeira on the profits, but they made off with everything, and I was the one who had to settle accounts. The case was closed years ago, but a certain urge for order made me hold on to these receipts, and now I don't want to carry them with me either.

"Well, I'll say goodbye. I'm going to take an empty barge to the Mártir Swamp, and if I pick up some passengers down-river, I'll have enough money to start again." He stood up and extended his hand with the gesture, part ceremonial, part military, that was so typical of him. Before I could urge him to stay the night and start downriver the next morning, he had disappeared into the coffee plantings, whistling a rather trite old song that had been the joy of our youth. I looked through his papers and found a good number of clues to the Gaviero's past life that he had never mentioned. Just then, down below, I heard the sound of his footsteps echoing against the zinc roof of the covered bridge that crosses the river. I felt his absence, and I began to recall his voice and gestures, and how much they had changed, and they came back to me now like an ominous warning that I would never see him again.

[E.G.]

Una calle de Córdoba

Para Leticia y Luis Feduchi

En una calle de Córdoba, una calle como tantas, con sus tiendas de postales y artículos para turistas,

una heladería y dos bares con mesas en la acera y en el interior chillones carteles de toros,

una calle con sus hondos zaguanes que desembocan en floridos jardines con su fuente de azulejos

y sus jaulas de pájaros que callan abrumados por el bochorno de la siesta,

uno que otro portón con su escudo de piedra y los borrosos signos de una abolida grandeza;

en una calle de Córdoba cuyo nombre no recuerdo o quizá nunca supe,

a lentos sorbos tomo una copa de jerez en la precaria sombra de la vereda.

Aquí y no en otra parte, mientras Carmen escoge en una tienda vecina las hermosas chilabas que regresan

después de cinco siglos para perpetuar la fresca delicia de la medina en los tiempos de Al-Andaluz,

en esta calle de Córdoba, tan parecida a tantas de Cartagena de Indias, de Antigua, de Santo Domingo o de la derruida Santa María del Darién,

aquí y no en otro lugar me esperaba la imposible, la ebria certeza de estar en España.

En España, a donde tantas veces he venido a buscar este instante, esta devastadora epifanía,

sucede el milagro y me interno lentamente en la felicidad sin término

rodeado de aromas, recuerdos, batallas, lamentos, pasiones sin salida,

por todos esos rostros, voces, airados reclamos, tiernos, dolientes ensalmos;

A Street in Córdoba

For Leticia y Luis Feduchi

In a street in Córdoba, a street like so many others, with its postcard and souvenir shops,

an ice-cream parlor and two bars with sidewalk tables and, inside, bullfight posters,

a street with deep entryways giving on to flowering gardens with a tiled fountain

and birds in cages, silent in the heavy heat of the siesta,

an occasional portico with its stone coat of arms and the fading trappings of an outworn grandeur;

in a street in Córdoba, whose name I no longer remember or perhaps never knew,

I sip at a sherry in the strip of shade on the sidewalk.

Here and in no other place, while Carmen in a neighboring shop picks out the elegant djellabas,

back in fashion after five centuries to perpetuate the cool pleasure of the medina in the times of Al-Andaluz,

in this street in Córdoba like so many others, in Cartagena de Indias, in Antigua, in Santo Domingo, or in the ruined Santa María in Darien,

here and in no other place the impossible was lying in wait for me, the heady certainty of being in Spain.

In Spain, where I have come SO many times, looking for this moment, this overwhelming epiphany,

the miracle happens, and slowly begin to bask in an endless joy,

surrounded by smells and memories, battles, laments, bottled-up passions,

by all those faces and voices, angry calls, gentle calls, woebegone spells;

I don't know how to put it, it is so difficult.

no sé cómo decirlo, es tan difícil.

Es la España de Abu-l-Hassan Al-Husri, "El Ciego", la del bachiller Sansón Carrasco,

la del príncipe Don Felipe, primogénito del César, que desembarca en Inglaterra todo vestido de blanco,

para tomar en matrimonio a María Tudor, su tía, y deslumbrar con sus maneras y elegancia a la corte inglesa,

la del joven oficial de albo coleto que parece pedir silencio en *Las lanzas* de Velázquez;

la España, en fin, de mi imposible amor por la Infanta Catalina Micaela, que con estrábico asombro

me mira desde su retrato en el Museo del Prado,

la España del chofer que hace poco nos decía: "El peligro está donde está el cuerpo."

Pero no es sólo esto, hay mucho más que se me escapa.

Desde niño he estado pidiendo, soñando, anticipando,

esta certeza que ahora me invade como una repentina temperatura, como un sordo golpe en la garganta,

aquí en esta calle de Córdoba, recostado en la precaria mesa de latón mientras saboreo el jerez

que como un ser vivo expande en mi pecho su calor generoso, su suave vértigo estival.

Aquí, en España, cómo explicarlo si depende de las palabras y éstas no son bastantes para conseguirlo.

Los dioses, en alguna parte, han consentido, en un instante de espléndido desorden,

que esto ocurra, que esto me suceda en una calle de Córdoba,

quizá porque ayer oré en el Mihrab de la Mezquita, pidiendo una señal que me entregase, así, sin motivo ni mérito alguno,

la certidumbre de que en esta calle, en esta ciudad, en los interminables olivares quemados al sol,

It is the Spain of Abu al-Hasan al-Husri, "The Blind One," of the scholar Samson Carrasco,

of Don Felipe, the prince, primogenitor of Caesar, who comes ashore in England dressed all in white

to take in marriage Mary Tudor, his aunt, and to dazzle the English court with his manners and his elegance,

of the young, white-vested officer who seems to be calling for silence in Velázquez's *Las Lanzas*;

the Spain, too, of my impossible love for the Infanta Catalina Micaela who, in cross-eyed astonishment,

looks down at me from her portrait in the Prado,

the Spain of the chauffeur who told us not long ago: "Danger is wherever the body is."

But not just that—there is much more that eludes me.

Since I was a child, I have been asking for, dreaming of, expecting

this certainty that now sweeps over me like a sudden high temperature, a silent gulp in the throat,

here, in this street, in Córdoba, leaning on this teetering brass table while I savor the sherry

that like a living thing spreads through me its generous warmth, its smooth summer vertigo.

Here, in Spain—how can I explain it in words, words unable to contain it.

The gods in some sense have agreed, in an instant of wondrous disorder,

that this should occur, that this should happen to me in a street in Córdoba,

perhaps because yesterday I prayed, in the Mihrab de la Mezquita, asking for a sign, just SO, without any reason or excuse,

the certainty that in this street, in this city, in the endless olive groves burnt by the sun,

en las colinas, las serranías, los ríos, las ciudades, los pueblos, los caminos, en España, en fin,

estaba el lugar, el único e insustituible lugar en donde todo se cumpliría para mí

con esta plenitud vencedora de la muerte y sus astucias, del olvido y del turbio comercio de los hombres.

Y ese don me ha sido otorgado en esta calle como tantas otras, con sus tiendas para turistas, su heladería, sus bares, sus portalones historiados,

en esta calle de Córdoba, donde el milagro ocurre, así, de pronto, como cosa de todos los días,

como un trueque del azar que le pago gozoso con las más negras horas de miedo y mentira,

de servil aceptación y de resignada desesperanza,

que han ido jalonando hasta hoy la apagada noticia de mi vida.

Todo se ha salvado ahora, en esta calle de la capital de los Omeyas pavimentada por los romanos,

en donde el Duque de Rivas moró en su palacio de catorce jardines y una alcoba regia para albergar a los reyes nuestros señores.

Concedo que los dioses han sido justos y que todo está, al fin, en orden.

Al terminar este jerez continuaremos el camino en busca de la pequeña sinagoga en donde meditó Maimónides

y seré, hasta el último día, otro hombre o, mejor, el mismo pero rescatado y dueño, desde hoy, de un lugar sobre la tierra.

in the hills, the *serranos*, the rivers, the cities, the villages, the roads, in Spain, finally,

was the place, the single, irreplaceable place where everything would come together for me

in this fullness that overcomes death and its devices, and forgetting, and the confused commerce of men.

And this gift has been granted me, in this street like so many others, with its tourist shops, its ice-cream parlor, its bars, its storied doorways,

in this street in Córdoba, where the miracle happens, just so, like something quite ordinary,

like a stroke of luck that I gladly pay for with my blackest hours of fear and betrayal,

of abject acceptance and of resigned despair,

which have marked the exhausted progress of my life, until today.

Everything has been redeemed now, in this street in the capital of the Omeyas, paved by the Romans,

where the Duke of Rivas lived, in his palace with fourteen gardens and royal quarters kept in readiness for kings.

I grant that the gods have been just and that everything at last is in order.

When I finish this sherry, we will go on looking for the little synagogue where Maimonides meditated,

and I will be until my very last day another man, or rather, the same one but now rescued, master, from today on, of a place on earth.

[A.R.]

Trítpico de la Alhambra

Para Santiago Mutis Durán

I. EN EL PARTAL

Hace tanto la música ha callado.
    Sólo el tiempo
        en las paredes, en las leves columnas
        en las inscripciones de los versos
        de Ibn Zamrak
        que celebran la hermosura del lugar,
    sólo el tiempo
        cumple su tarea
        con leve
        sordo roce
        sin pausa ni destino.
Al fondo,
ajenos a toda mudanza,
el Albaicín
y las pardas colinas de olivares.
    Carmen lanza migas de pan
        en el estanque
        y los peces acuden en un tropel
        de escamas desteñidas por los años.
Inclinada sobre el agua,
sonríe al desorden que ha creado
    y su sonrisa,
    con la tenue tristeza que la empaña,
suscita la improbable maravilla:
en un presente de exacta plenitud
vuelven los días de Yusuf,
el Nasrí,
en el ámbito intacto de la Alhambra.

Alhambra Triptych

For Santiago Mutis Durán

I. IN THE PARTAL PALACE

The music fell silent so long ago.
    Time alone
        in the walls, in the slender columns,
        in the lines of Ibn Zamrak
        inscribed
        to celebrate the beauty of this place
    time alone
        performs its task
        of delicate
        hushed erosion,
        unrelenting and aimless.
Beyond,
indifferent to all change,
the Albaicín
and the dun, olive-covered hills.
    Carmen scatters bread crumbs
        on the pond,
        and the fish rise in a surge
        of scales faded by the years.
Bent over the water
she smiles at the fray she has created
    and her smile
    with its fine mist of sadness
brings on the improbable wonder:
In a moment of exact plenitude,
the days of Yusuf
the Nasrid
return
to the intact ambit of the Alhambra.

2. UN GORRIÓN ENTRA AL MEXUAR

Entre un tropel y otro de turistas
la calma ceremoniosa vuelve al Mexuar.
El sol se demora en el piso y un tibio silencio
se expande por el ámbito donde embajadores, visires,
funcionarios, solicitantes, soplones y guerreros
fueron oídos antaño por el Comendador de los Creyentes.
Por una de las ventanas que dan al jardín
entra un gorrión que a saltos se desplaza
con la tranquila seguridad de quien se sabe
dueño sin émulo de los lugares.
Vuelve hacia nosotros la cabeza
y sus ojos—dos rayos de azabache—
nos miran con altanero descuido.
En su agitado paseo por la sala
hay una energía apenas contenida,
un dominio de quien está más allá
de los torpes intrusos que nada saben
de la teoría de reverencias, órdenes, oraciones,
tortuosos amores y ejecuciones sumarias,
que rige en estos parajes en donde la ajena incuria,
propia de la triste familia de los hombres,
ha impuesto hoy su oscuro designio, su voluntad de olvido.
Vuela el gorrión entre el laborioso artesonado
y afirma, en la minuciosa certeza de sus desplazamientos,
su condición de soberano detentador
de los más ocultos y vastos poderes.
Celador sin sosiego de un pasado abolido
nos deja de súbito relegados al mísero presente
de invasores sin rostro, sin norte, sin consigna.
Irrumpe el rebaño de turistas. Se ha roto el encanto.
El gorrión escapa hacia el jardín.
Y he aquí que, por obra de un velado sortilegio

2. A SPARROW COMES INTO THE MEXUAR

Between one mob of tourists and the next
stately calm returns to the Mexuar.
Sunlight lingers on the floor, and warm silence
dilates in the space where ambassadors, viziers,
officials, petitioners, informers, and warriors
were once granted an audience
by the Commander of the Faithful.
Through one of the windows facing the garden
a sparrow comes hopping in
with the calm confidence of one who is sure
of his unchallenged claim to dominion.
He turns his head toward us
and his eyes—two jet-black rays—
watch us with a grand indifference.
In his flurried tour of the room
there is a barely contained energy,
a self-possession that sets him apart
from the clumsy intruders, unschooled
in the protocol of bows, commands, prayers,
star-crossed loves, and summary executions
proper to this site, where the disregard
native to the sorry human family
has now enacted its dark plan, its will to oblivion.
The sparrow flies around the elaborate coffered ceiling,
and the precise assurance of his movements
confirms his status as sovereign possessor
of the most hidden and far-reaching powers.
Tireless guardian of an abolished past,
he abandons us abruptly to the wretched present
of faceless, aimless, ill-prepared invaders.
The flock of tourists presses in. The charm is broken.
The sparrow escapes into the garden.

los severos, autoritarios gestos del inquieto centinela
me han traído de pronto la pálida suma
de encuentros, muertes, olvidos y derogaciones,
el suplicio de máscaras y mezquinas alegrías
que son la vida y su agria ceniza segadora.
Pero también han llegado,
en la dorada plenitud de ese instante,
las fieles señales que, a mi favor,
rescatan cada día el ávido tributo de la tumba:
mi padre que juega billar en el café Lion D'Or de Bruselas,
las calles recién lavadas camino del colegio en la mañana,
el olor del mar en el verano de Ostende,
el amigo que murió en mis brazos cuando asistíamos al
        circo,
la adolescente que me miró distraída mientras
colgaba a secar la ropa al fondo de un patio de naranjos,
las últimas páginas de *Victory* de Joseph Conrad,
las tardes en la hacienda de Coello con su cálida tiniebla
        repentina,
el aura de placer y júbilo que despide la palabra Marianao,
la voz de Ernesto enumerando la sucesión de soberanos
        sálicos,
la contenida, firme, insomne voz de Gabriel en una sala de
        Estocolmo,
Nicolás señalando las virtudes de la prosa de Taine,
la sonrisa de Carmen ayer en el estanque del Partal;
éstas y algunas otras dádivas que los años
nos van reservando con terca parsimonia
desfilaron convocadas por la sola maravilla
del gorrión de mirada insolente y gestos de monarca,
dueño y señor en el Mexuar de la Alhambra.

And now, by the power of a secret spell,
that restless sentry's curt, commanding gestures
have suddenly recalled the bloodless sum
of encounters, deaths, omissions, abolitions,
painful masquerades, and petty joys
that go to make life and its bitter, blinding ash.
But the faithful signs have also come
in that moment's golden plenitude
to redeem as they do every day
the greedy taxes of the tomb:
My father playing billiards in the Lion d'Or café in
    Brussels,
the freshly washed streets on the way to school in the
    morning,
the smell of the sea in Ostend in summer,
the friend who died in my arms at the circus,
the girl who gazed at me absently
while hanging out washing in an orange-tree courtyard,
the final pages of Joseph Conrad's *Victory*,
evenings on the estate in Coello, the warm night falling
    suddenly,
the aura of pleasure and delight given off by the word
    "Marianao,"
Ernesto's voice running through the sovereigns according
    to the Salic law,
Gabriel's measured, steady, sleepless voice in a hall in
    Stockholm,
Nicolas detailing the merits of Taine's prose,
Carmen's smile yesterday at the pond in the Partal Palace;
these and other gifts, which the years
with stubborn parsimony hold in store,
filed past, called up simply by the wonder
of a brazen-eyed sparrow with the bearing of a monarch,
lord and master in the Mexuar of the Alhambra.

3. EN LA ALCAZABA

El desnudo rigor castrense de estos muros,
tintos de herrumbre y llaga, sin inscripciones
que celebren su historia, mudos
en el adusto olvido de anónimos guerreros,
sólo consigue evocar la rancia rutina
de la guerra, esa muerte sin rostro,
ese cansado trajín de las armas,
las mañanas a la espera de las huestes
africanas, cuya algarabía ensordece
y abre paso a un pánico que pronto
ha de tornarse vértigo de ira sin esclusas
y así hasta cuando llega la noche
sembrada de hogueras, relinchos y susurros
que prometen para el alba un nuevo
y fastidioso trasiego con la sangre
que escurre en el piso como una savia
lenta, como un torpe y viscoso camino
de infortunio. Y un día un aroma de naranjos,
las voces de mujeres que bajan al río
para lavar sus ropas y bañarse,
el vaho que sube de las cocinas y huele
a cordero, a laurel y a especias capitosas,
el sol en las almenas y el jubiloso restallar
de las insignias, anuncian el fin de la brega
y el retiro de los imprevisibles sitiadores.
Y así un año y otro año
y un siglo y otro siglo,
hasta dejar en estos aposentos,
donde resuena la voz del visitante
en la húmeda penumbra sin memoria,
en estos altos muros oxidados de sangre
y liquen y ajenos también e indescifrables,

3. IN THE ALCAZABA

The naked military rigor of these walls,
scarred, bleeding rust, without inscriptions
to celebrate their history, dumb
in their bleak disregard for nameless warriors,
can summon only the archaic routine
of war, that faceless death,
that weary commotion of arms,
mornings waiting for the hosts
from Africa, their deafening uproar
triggering a panic soon transformed
into a frenzy of unchecked wrath
continuing until the fall of a night
strewn with fires, whinnying, and whispers,
which promise for the dawn ahead
yet another outpouring of blood
that oozes over the floor like slow
sap, like a blundering, sticky path
to disaster. Then one day a fragrance of oranges,
voices of women going down to the river
to wash their clothes and bathe,
vapors rising from the kitchens with scents
of lamb, bay leaves, and heady spices,
sun on the battlements, and the joyful snap
of banners, all announcing the end of the strife
and the surprise retreat of the siege force.
And so on year after year,
century after century,
gradually depositing a trace
in these chambers where the visitor's voice
echoes in the damp, amnesiac half-light
on these high walls stained with blood and lichen,
alien, too, and inscrutable,

esa vaga huella de muchas voces,
de silencios agónicos, de nostalgias
de otras tierras y otros cielos,
que son el pan cotidiano de la guerra,
el único y ciego signo del soldado
que se pierde en el vano servicio de las armas,
pasto del olvido, vocación de la nada.

a faint trace of many voices,
of dying silences, of the longings
for other lands and other skies
that are the daily bread of war,
the sole, blind sign of the soldier lost
in the futile exercise of arms,
fed to oblivion, called to nothingness.

[C.A.]

The Aracuriare Canyon

To understand the effect on the Gaviero's life of the time he spent in the Aracuriare Canyon, one must consider certain features of a place that is usually deserted because it is far from any road or trail used by people from the low country, and because it has a dismal reputation, which, although not entirely undeserved, still does not correspond to its true image.

The river rushes down from the cordillera in a torrent of icy water that crashes against boulders and treacherous shoals, creating a frenzy of foam and whirlpools and the wild, furious roar of an unrestrained current. It is thought that the river carries sands heavy with gold, and prospectors often make precarious camp at its edge and wash the earth along the bank, but so far there have been no significant finds. Hopelessness soon overwhelms these outsiders, and local fevers and plagues make short work of their lives. The constant humid heat and a scarcity of food finish off those who are not accustomed to the burning climate. Such undertakings usually end in a rosary of humble mounds, resting places for the bones of men who never knew rest or tranquillity in life. The river begins to slow when it enters a narrow valley, and the water acquires a smooth, peaceful surface that hides the dense energy of the current, free at last from all obstacles. At the end of the valley looms an imposing mass of granite split in two by a dark cleft. This is where the river, in a silent rush of water as solemn as a processional, penetrates the shadowy canyon. The interior, formed by walls that rise straight up to the sky, their surface covered by a sparse growth of lianas and ferns struggling to reach the sun, has the air of an abandoned cathedral, a half-light disturbed from time to time by sparrow hawks that nest in the narrow crevices of

the rock, or flocks of parrots whose screeches fill the canyon with a nerve-shattering din that brings one's oldest longings back to life.

The river has created a few slate-colored beaches that glisten during the brief intervals when sunlight reaches the bottom of the canyon. Usually the water's surface is so serene that the movement of the current can hardly be detected. Only an occasional bubbling can be heard, ending in a vague sigh, a kind of profound complaint that rises from the depths and betrays the immense, treacherous energy hidden in the river's peaceful flow.

The Gaviero traveled there to deliver the instruments, scales, and mercury ordered by a pair of prospectors with whom he had contracted in an oil port on the coast. When he arrived he learned that his customers had died several weeks earlier and been buried by a charitable soul at the entrance to the canyon. Their names were written on a worm-eaten board in an improbable orthography that the Gaviero could hardly decipher. He entered the canyon and walked the smooth, broad beaches, where he occasionally saw a bird skeleton or the remains of a raft carried there by the current from a distant settlement further up the valley.

The warm monastic silence, its isolation from all human disorder and tumult, and an intense, insistent call impossible to put into words or even thoughts, were enough to make the Gaviero feel a desire to stay for a time, if only to escape the noisy traffic in the ports and the contrary star of his insatiable wandering.

With pieces of wood collected along the shore and palm leaves pulled from the current, he built a hut on a slate shoal that rose at the end of the beach where he decided to live. The fruits continually washed down by the river and the birds he caught without difficulty were his food.

The days passed, and with no particular purpose in mind

the Gaviero began an examination of his life, a catalogue of his miseries, his mistakes, his precarious joys and confused passions. He resolved to go deep into this task, and his success was so thorough and devastating that he rid himself completely of the self who had accompanied him all his life, the one who had suffered all the pain and difficulty. He moved ahead in the search for his own frontiers, his true limits, and when he saw the protagonist of what he had always considered his own life recede and disappear, all that remained was the self engaged in the scrutiny, the act of simplification. He persisted in his effort to learn more about the new man born of his deepest essence, and a mixture of astonishment and joy suddenly overwhelmed him, for a third, impassive spectator was waiting for him, taking form and shape in the very center of his being. He was convinced that this self, who had never taken part in any of the episodes of his life, must know all the truth, all the pathways, all the motives, that had woven his destiny, which he could see now with naked clarity, and he realized suddenly that it was entirely useless and worthy only of rejection. But as he faced that absolute witness of himself, he also felt the serene, ameliorating acceptance he had spent so many years searching for in the fruitless symbols of adventure.

Until that confrontation, the Gaviero had gone through arduous periods of searching and testing and making many false discoveries in the canyon. The atmosphere with its resonance of a basilica, and the ocher blanket of water moving with hypnotic slowness, were confused in his memory with the internal movement that carried him toward this third, impassive sentinel of his existence, who did not judge, either to praise or condemn, who did no more than observe him with an otherworldly intensity that in turn reflected, like a mirror, the astonished passing of the moments of Maqroll's life. Serenity tinged with a kind of feverish pleasure

invaded him, anticipating that portion of joy which we all hope to achieve before we die but which recedes as the years advance and the despair they bring with them increases.

The Gaviero felt that if the plenitude he had just attained could continue, death would lack all importance and be simply one more episode in the script, accepted as easily as one turns a corner or rolls over in bed while sleeping. For Maqroll the granite walls, the lazy flow of water, the smooth surfaces and echoing emptiness of the canyon, were like a premonitory image of the kingdom of forgotten men, the domain where death mingles with the procession of her sleepless creatures.

Since he knew that from then on the way things happened would be very different from what it had been in the past, the Gaviero delayed leaving, put off joining in the clamor of men. He was afraid to disturb his newly won tranquillity. Finally, one day, he tied some balsa trunks into a raft with vines, reached the middle of the current, and sailed downriver through the narrow gorge. A week later he emerged into the white light of the delta where the river empties into a calm, warm sea, and a light mist rises that makes distance more remote and expands the horizon into endless extension.

He spoke to no one of his time in the Aracuriare Canyon. What is written here was taken from notes discovered in the armoire of the miserable hotel room where he spent his last days before leaving for the marshlands.

[E.G.]

Noticia del Hades

Para Jaime Jaramillo Escobar

"Seul, ton néant est éternel."
—Paul Léautaud

El calor me despertó en medio de la noche
y bajé a la quebrada en busca de la fresca brisa
que viene de los páramos. Sentado bajo un frondoso guadual
un hombre esperaba, oculto en la esbelta sombra de las
    matas.
Permaneció en silencio hasta cuando le pregunté
quién era y qué hacía allí. Se levantó para responderme
y desde la oscuridad vegetal que lo ocultaba llegó su voz
y sus palabras tenían la afelpada independencia,
el opaco acento de una región inconcebible.
"Vengo —me dijo— de las heladas parcelas de la muerte,
de los dominios donde el cisne surca las aguas serenas
y preside el silencio de los que allí han llegado
para esperar, en medio de las altas paredes de granito,
la inefable señal, la siempre esperada y siempre postergada
señal de su definitiva disolución en la nada bienhechora.
Ni la pulida superficie de las rocas, ni el helado espejo
de las aguas, guardan signo alguno de esa presencia innu-
    merable.
Sólo la nielada estela del perpetuo navegar
del ave que vigila y recorre esas regiones, anuncia
cuáles son los poderes y quiénes los habitantes que pueblan
el ámbito sin designio ni evasión del que vengo a dar
    noticia.
Cada cual existe allí por obra de su propio y desolado
apartamiento. Sólo el cisne, en su tránsito sin pausa,
con breves giros de su albo cuello majestuoso,
nos reúne bajo el mismo gesto de un hierático despojo.

News from Hades

For Jaime Jaramillo Escobar

"Seul, ton néant est éternel."
—Paul Léautaud

The heat woke me in the middle of the night,
and I went down to the gorge in search of a breeze
from the plains. Sitting beneath a leafy bamboo,
a man was waiting, hidden in the thin shade of the trees.
He kept silent until the moment I asked him
who he was, what he was doing there. He rose to answer,
and his voice came out of the vegetal dark that hid him.
His words had a smooth and independent edge,
and the opaque accent of an unimaginable region.
"I come," he said, "from the frozen plots of death,
from domains where the swan furrows the placid waters
and silence rules, the silence of those who have come
to wait, among the towering walls of granite, for the sign,
    always expected, always delayed,
the ineffable sign of their final dissolution
into the blessing of nothingness.
Neither the smooth rock face nor the frozen mirror
of the waters retain any sign of that crowded presence.
Only the inlaid wake from the endless courses
of the bird that watches and patrols those regions
lays down the people and powers that inhabit that state,
with neither hope nor escape, that I come to tell you of.
Each one there exists in the desolation
of his own solitude. Only the swan, in its endless passing,
with faint movements of its wondrous white neck,
unites us under the gesture of princely authority.
The silent wind, blowing faintly from granite peaks,
is not enough to trouble the lake water. It arrives

La brisa callada que baja a menudo de las cimas de granito
no basta para inquietar la superficie del lago. Nos llega
como una última llamada del mundo de los vivos,
de ese mundo en donde apuras, en distraído goce,
los dones que nosotros, allá, en nuestros parajes,
ya hemos olvidado. Observa cómo ninguna piedra es
muda en este tu mundo. Aquí te acogen voces, ecos y
    llamadas
todo te nombra, todo existe para tu protección y alivio.
Como presente no pedido y que no mereces vine a revelarte
lo que te espera. No saques apresuradas conclusiones,
nada de lo que puedas hacer se tendrá en cuenta
entre nosotros. La estancada y dura transparencia
de nuestro reino no es propicia a los recuerdos y esperanzas
que tejes y destejes en el tropel sin norte de tus días.
No creo que llegues a entender lo que he narrado.
Pertenece a una materia y a un tiempo que sólo los muertos
tenemos la lenta y gélida paciencia de habitar.
La huella del cisne sobre las aguas nos mantiene
a la espera de nada, apartados y ajenos, presos
en la neutra mirada del centinela de radiante blancura
en cuyos ojos se repite la teoría de los acantilados
que a trechos macula el óxido estéril de un liquen inmu-
    table."
Esto dijo y al extender la mano desde la tibia penumbra,
pareció iniciar un gesto ambiguo con el cual, a tiempo
que se despedía, me indicaba que, en alguna forma,
para mí indescifrable, yo me estaba iniciando en sus
    dominios.

like a last summons from the world of the living,
this world in which you use up, pleasure-minded,
the gifts that we, down there, in our condition,
have already forgotten. Notice: in this world of yours,
no stone is mute. Here, voices welcome you, echoes and
     greetings
all name you. All exists to protect and comfort you.
Like a present unasked for, undeserved, I came to reveal
what is in store for you. Do not draw hasty conclusions.
Nothing you can do will count at all with us.
The stagnant, hard transparency of our kingdoms
does not encourage the hopes and memories
you weave and unweave in the aimless movement of days.
I don't think you begin to grasp what I've told you.
It belongs to a matter and time that only we dead
have the slow and icy patience to inhabit.
The wake of the swan on the waters keeps us hoping
for nothing, separate, alien, and imprisoned
in the neutral gaze of the radiant white sentry
in whose eyes is repeated the message of the cliffs
stained in places by the sterile oxide of immutable lichen."
So did he speak; and, reaching his hand from the half-dark,
he made, as he said farewell, an ambiguous gesture
as if to let me know that, in some way that escaped me,
he was initiating me into his dominions.

[A.R.]

Estela para Arthur Rimbaud

Señor de las arenas,
recorres tus dominios
y desde el mirador
de la torre más alta
parten tus órdenes
que van a perderse
en el sordo vacío
del estuario.
Señor de las armas
ilusorias, hace tanto
que el olvido trabaja
tus poderes,
que tu nombre, tu reino,
la torre, el estuario,
las arenas y las armas
se borraron para siempre
del gastado tapiz
que las narraba.
No agites más
tus raídos estandartes.
En la quietud, en el silencio,
has de internarte
abandonado
a tus redes funerales.

Stela for Arthur Rimbaud

Lord of the sands,
you survey your domains,
and from the mirador
of the highest tower
your orders go forth
only to be lost
in the deaf emptiness
of the estuary.
Lord of the illusory
arms, it is so long
since forgetting set to work
on your powers,
since your name, your kingdom,
the tower, the estuary,
the sands, and the arms
were forever effaced
from the worn tapestry
that told their tale.
Stop brandishing
your threadbare standards.
Into stillness, into silence
you must venture,
given over
to your funereal webs.

[C.A.]

Homenaje

Después de escuchar la música de Mario Lavista

El aire se serena y viste de hermosura y
luz no usada.
　　　—Fray Luis de León

Ni aquel que con la sola virtud de su mirada
detiene el deslizamiento de los glaciares
suspensos, por un instante, en su desmesurada
blancura, antes del alud desbocado
en el vértigo de sus destrucciones.
Ni aquel que alza un fruto partido por la mitad
y lo ofrece a la vasta soledad del cielo
en donde el sol establece
su abrasadora labor a la hora de la siesta.
Ni aquel que mide con minuciosa exactitud
los espacios del aire, las zonas donde la muerte
acecha con su ciega jauría y que es el mismo
que maneja la espada y reconoce
en las manchas irisadas de la hoja
un veredicto inapelable, instantáneo y certero.
Ni aquel que implora una limosna
bajo los altos soportales de piedra
en donde el eco repite sus súplicas,
libres de la vanidosa aflicción del pudor.
Ni aquel que sube a los trenes
sabiendo que no ha de volver
porque el regreso es un espejismo deleznable.
Ni aquel que acecha al amanecer el paso
de raudas migraciones que, por un instante,
pueblan el cielo con la sombra de su tránsito,
anunciador de monzones y de pardas desventuras.
Ni aquel que dice saber y calla
y con su silencio apenas logra alejarnos

Homage

After listening to the music of Mario Lavista

> *"The air grows calm and puts on beauty and*
> *unaccustomed light."*
>> —Fray Luis de León

Not who by the sole power of a gaze
holds the sliding glaciers
still for a moment in their immense
whiteness, before the avalanche tears loose
in a vertigo of destruction.
Nor who raises a fruit cut in half
and offers it to the sky's vast solitude
where the sun instates
its burning toil at the hour of the siesta.
Nor who measures with meticulous precision
the spaces of the air, the zones where death
lies in wait with its blind hounds, and who also
wields the sword and discerns
a verdict—final, immediate, and sound—
in the blade's iridescent stains.
Nor who begs for alms
in the stone arcade
where an echo repeats entreaties
free of the vain affliction of shame.
Nor who boards trains
knowing the journey is one-way
because return is a frail mirage.
Nor who watches at dawn
for the rushing migrant flocks that fill the sky
for a moment with the darkness of their passage,
presaging monsoons and somber misadventures.
Nor who claims to know and says nothing,
whose silence can barely preserve us

de estériles maquinaciones sin salida.
Ni ningún otro que intente exhibir
ante nosotros la más especiosa y letal
de esas destrezas que le son dadas
al hombre para orientar el sino
de sus disoluciones y mudanzas.
Nadie, en fin, conseguirá evocar
la despojada maravilla de esta música
limpia de las más imperceptibles huellas
de nuestra perecedera voluntad de canto.
De espaldas al mundo, al polvo,
al tibio remolino de nostalgias y sueños
y de efímeras representaciones,
esta leve fábrica se levanta
por el solo milagro de haber vencido
al tiempo y a sus más recónditas argucias.
Apenas escuchada, se transforma,
cambia de lugar y nos sorprende
desde un rincón donde jamás
sospechamos que se diera.
No tiene signo este don de una eternidad
y que, sin pertenecernos, nos rescata
del uso y las costumbres,
de los días y del llanto,
del gozo y su ceniza voladora.
Imposible saber en qué parcela del azar
agazapada esta música destila
su instantáneo licor de transparencia
y nos lleva al borde de un océano
que sin cesar recrea en sus orillas
la dorada permanencia de las formas.
Del diálogo del cristal y del oboe,
de lo que el clarinete propone como huida
y la flauta regresa a sus dominios,

from sterile machinations without issue.
Nor anyone else who attempts to impress
with the most specious and lethal of the skills
granted us to orient the course
of our dissolutions and changes.
No one, in sum, will be able to evoke
the pared-back wonder of this music
free of the most imperceptible trace
of our perishable will to song.
With its back to the world, to dust,
to the tepid swirling of nostalgia, dreams,
and ephemeral representations,
this delicate factory builds itself
by the sole miracle of its triumph
over time and its most cryptic sophistries.
Almost as soon as heard it changes,
shifts, and surprises us
from a corner where we would never
have imagined it might arise.
No sign limits this gift of an eternity
that rescues us, without being ours,
from habit and custom,
from days and tears,
from pleasure and its flyaway ash.
No knowing in which sector of chance
this music lies hidden, distilling
its instant spirit of transparency,
taking us to the edge of an ocean
which ceaselessly recreates on its shores
the golden permanence of the forms.
What glass and oboe say to each other,
what flight the clarinet proposes,
what the flute brings home to its domains,
what the strings offer as enigma

de lo que las cuerdas ofrecen como enigma
y ellas mismas devuelven a la nada,
sólo el silencio guarda la memoria.
No sabemos y en nuestra conquistada resignación
tal vez está el secreto de ese instante
otorgado por los dioses
como una prueba de nuestra obediencia
a un orden donde el tiempo ha perdido
la engañosa condición de sus poderes.

and then give back to nothingness,
only silence holds in memory.
We do not know, and in our hard-won resignation
lies, perhaps, the secret of that moment
bestowed upon us by the gods
like proof of our obedience
to an order in which time has lost
the fraudulent standing of its powers.

[C.A.]

Nocturno I

La tenue luz de esa lámpara
en la noche débilmente
se debate con las sombras
No alcanza a rozar los muros
ni a penetrar en la tiniebla
sin límites del techo
Por el suelo avanza
No logra abrirse paso
más allá de su reino intermitente
restringido al breve ámbito
de sus oscilaciones
Al alba termina
su duelo con la noche
la astuta tejedora
en su blanda trama
de hollín y desamparo
Como un pálido aviso
del mundo de los vivos
esa luz apenas presente
ha bastado
para devolvernos a la mansa
procesión de los días
a su blanca secuencia
de horas muertas
De su terca vigilia
de su clara batalla
con la sombra sólo queda
de esa luz vencida
la memoria de su vana proeza
Así las palabras buscando
presintiendo el exacto lugar

Nocturne I

The fitful glow of that lamp
every night at nightfall
takes on the dark
It scarcely tints the wall
or penetrates the deepening
darkness of the ceiling
Its light across the floor
can reach no further
than its own fixed space
the compass of its tentative
lamp-lit territory
Dawn brings a daily end to
that duel with the darkness
skillfully weaving
with masterful design
the dark with its undoing
Like a ghostly warning
from the world of the living
that first glimmer of daylight
does just enough
to turn us back to the usual
shifting of the days
in their steady sequence
of used-up hours
All that remains
of the stubborn vigilance
of that defeated lamp
in its daily battle
with darkness is the memory
of its sheer persistence—
just as certain words

que las espera en el frágil
maderamen del poema
por designio inefable
de los dioses.

find the appointed place
almost as if predestined
that waits for them in the fragile
scaffolding of the poem
fulfilling the ineffable
design of the gods.

[A.R.]

Nocturno III

Había avanzado la noche hasta establecer sus dominios
acallando apagando todo rumor todo ruido
que no fueran propios de su expandida tiniebla
de sus tortuosas galerías de sus lentos laberintos
por los que se avanza dando tumbos contra blandas paredes
donde rebota el eco de palabras y pasos de otros días
y flotan y se acercan y se alejan rostros
disueltos en el hollín impalpable del sueño
rostros que nos visitaron en la infancia
o que encontramos un día cualquiera
en los anónimos pasillos de un ministerio
o en el lavabo de una estación de tren abandonada
o junto a una mujer que tal vez hubiera cambiado nuestra
      vida
y con la que nunca hablamos ni supimos su nombre
y que tomaba lentamente un vaso de leche tibia
en el sórdido rincón de un café de provincia
en donde el ruido de las bolas de billar
se mezclaba con la gangosa música de un tocadiscos
o en la pulcra oficina de correos de Namur
a donde fuimos por un paquete de ultramar
Porque la noche reserva
esas sorpresas destinadas a quienes saben negociar
con sus poderes y perderse en sus corredores
habiendo abandonado por completo las precarias
armas que concede la vigilia y violado la limitada
tolerancia con la que nos permite internarnos
en ciertas regiones sin dejar de ejercer
sobre nosotros sus decretos de ceniza ni de extender
a nuestro paso la raída alfombra de sus concesiones
Pocos son en verdad los elegidos que se libran

Nocturne III

Advancing night had taken control
silencing stifling all chatter all clamor
alien to its dilated darkness
its winding passages and slow mazes
in which one blunders into soft walls
and the words and steps of other days echo
and faces float and approach and recede
dispersed in the intangible ash of dreams
faces that visited us in childhood
or that we met on some ordinary day
in the anonymous corridors of a ministry
or the restroom of a disused train station
or beside a woman who might have changed our lives
to whom we never spoke whose name we never knew
who was sipping a glass of warm milk
in the dingy corner of a provincial café
where the clacking of billiard balls
punctuated the nasal tunes of a record player
or in the immaculate post office in Namur
where we went to collect a package from overseas
Because the night holds these surprises
in store for those who know how to parley
with its powers and lose themselves in its corridors
having completely abandoned the puny
arms afforded by the waking state and breached
the limits within which it tolerates
our incursions into certain regions
while still enforcing its ashen decrees and rolling
the threadbare carpet of concessions out before us
Few in truth are the chosen who break free
of those shackles and venture into the night

de tales trabas y se lanzan a la noche con el afán
de quien intenta aprovechar plenamente esas vacaciones
sin término que el oscuro prestigio de sus reinos propone
como quien regala una aleatoria eternidad
una supervivencia sin garantía pero provista en cambio
de una módica cuota de tentadoras encrucijadas
en donde el placer se nos viene encima
con la felina presteza de lo que ha de perderse
Porque tiene radas la noche
dársenas tenuemente iluminadas móviles vegetaciones
de algas ansiosas que nos acogen meciendo
pausadamente sus telones cambiantes sus velos funerales
Y es por eso que quienes han sellado el pacto
suelen preparar con minucia y prudente entusiasmo
cada excursión por los reinos nocturnos
Como esos viajeros que guardan una botella de vino
que se bebió para despedir a quienes fueron a la guerra
y en las tardes la llenan de nuevo con aceite de palma
y sudor recogido en las sienes de los agonizantes
o como esos maquinistas que antes de emprender la partida
y acumular presión en las calderas graban en las paredes
de las mismas la oración de los pastores sin ganado
Pero tampoco es esto porque aquel que se instala
tras las fronteras de la noche no precisa ajustarse
a reglas tan rígidas ni a condiciones tan específicas
Es más bien como un dejarse llevar por la corriente
intentando apenas con un leve sacudir de las piernas
o con una brazada oportuna impedir el golpe
contra las piedras y ceder al impulso de las aguas
sin perder nunca una cierta autonomía
No para escapar al fin sino para que el descenso tenga
más de viaje sujeto a los caprichos del deseo
que de vértigo impuesto por las aguas
Pero tampoco es esto así porque la noche misma

with the thirst of one determined to take
full advantage of the endless vacation
promised by the dark prestige of its kingdoms
like the gift of a contingent eternity
a survival without guarantees but supplied
with a modest share of tempting forks
in the road where pleasure springs upon us
with the catlike swiftness of the soon-to-be-lost
Because the night has roadsteads
feebly lit docks a shifting vegetation
of eager seaweed that takes us in gently
swaying its changeable curtains its funeral veils
And that is why those who have sealed the pact
will prepare each excursion to the kingdoms of night
in detail and with cautious fervor
Like those travelers who keep a wine bottle
that was emptied to see off soldiers bound for war
and fill it again in the evenings with palm oil
and sweat mopped from the temples of the dying
or those engine drivers who before building up
a head of steam inscribe on the boiler's side
the prayer of the shepherd without a flock
But that is not quite right because the settler
beyond night's borders has no need to conform
to such strict rules or specific conditions
It is more like surrendering to the current
and trying with just a slight kick of the legs
or a well-timed stroke of the arms to steer clear
of the rocks and submitting to the water's force
without ever losing a certain autonomy
Not to escape in the end but to make the descent
more like a journey governed by the whims of desire
than a turmoil thrust upon us by the waters
But that is still not right because night itself

va dejando trampas por las que podemos escapar
de repente y es en el trabajo de presentirlas y evitarlas
cuando corremos el riesgo de perder lo mejor de la jornada
Por eso lo indicado es dejar una delgada zona de la conciencia
a cargo de esa tarea y lanzar el resto
a la plenitud de los poderes nocturnos
con la certeza siempre de que en ellos
hemos de errar sin sosiego sin cuidar que allí
acecha una falacia porque no existe prueba
de que nadie haya podido evitar el regreso.

leaves trapdoors through which we can suddenly escape
and if we are busy foreseeing and avoiding them
we could well be missing the best of the day
So it is wise to leave a slim fringe of consciousness
in charge of that task and give the rest over
to the nocturnal powers in their fullness
knowing all the while that in their realm
we must wander restlessly ignoring
the fallacy lurking there for nothing proves
that anyone has eluded the return.

[C.A.]

Nocturno en Valdemosa

A Jan Zych

"le silence... tu peux crier... le silence encore."
—*Carta de Chopin al poeta Mickiewicz
desde Valdemosa*

La tramontana azota en la noche
las copas de los pinos.
Hay una monótona insistencia
en ese viento demente y terco
que ya les habían anunciado en Port Vendres.
La tos se ha calmado al fin pero la fiebre queda
como un aviso aciago, inapelable,
de que todo ha de acabar en un plazo que se agota
con premura que no estaba prevista.
No halla sosiego y gimen las correas
que sostienen el camastro desde el techo.
Sobre los tejados de pizarra,
contra los muros del jardín oculto en la tiniebla,
insiste el viento como bestia acosada
que no encuentra la salida y se debate
agotando sus fuerzas sin remedio.
El insomnio establece sus astucias
y echa a andar la veloz devanadera:
regresa todo lo aplazado y jamás cumplido,
las músicas para siempre abandonadas
en el laberinto de lo posible,
en el paciente olvido acogedor.
El más arduo suplicio tal vez sea
el necio absurdo del viaje
en busca de un clima más benigno
para terminar en esta celda,
alto féretro donde la humedad
traza vagos mapas que la fiebre

Nocturne in Valdemosa

To Jan Zych

"le silence...tu peux crier...le silence encore."
—*Letter sent from Valdemosa by Chopin
to the poet Mickiewicz*

At night the north wind whips
the tops of the pines.
There is a monotonous insistence
in that stubborn and demented wind
that they had been forewarned of in Port Vendres.
His cough is quiet at last but the fever stays,
like a gloomy and dispiriting announcement
that everything must be finished by a deadline
that approaches with an unimagined haste.
He finds no peace. Even the leather straps
that support his wretched bed groan with him.
Over the roof-slates,
against the garden walls hidden in half-light,
the wind insists, a hunted beast
that can find no way out and turns on itself,
sapping its strength without surcease.
Insomnia sets up its own deceptions
and sets in motion an unwinding reel:
all that has been put off and never finished
comes back—the music left behind forever
in the vast labyrinth of the possible,
in the obedient shelter of forgetting.
The most corrosive torture may well be
the folly and absurdity of a journey
in quest of a climate more propitious
ending up in this cell,
a lofty coffin where the mildew
leaves phantom maps that fever

insiste en descifrar sin conseguirlo.
El musgo crea en el piso
una alfombra resbalosa
de sepulcro abandonado.
Por entre el viento y la vigilia
irrumpe la instantánea certeza
de que esta torpe aventura participa
del variable signo que ha enturbiado
cada momento de su vida.
Hasta el incomparable edificio de su obra
se desvanece y pierde por entero
toda presencia, toda razón, todo sentido.
Regresar a la nada se le antoja
un alivio, un bálsamo oscuro y eficaz
que los dioses ofrecen compasivos.
La voz del viento trae
la llamada febril que lo procura
desde esa otra orilla donde el tiempo
no reina ni ejerce ya poder alguno
con la hiel de sus conjuras y maquinaciones.
La tramontana se aleja, el viento calla
y un sordo grito se apaga en la garganta del insomne.
Al silencio responde otro silencio,
el suyo, el de siempre, el mismo
del que aún brotará por breve plazo
el delgado manantial de su música
a ninguna otra parecida y que nos deja
la nostalgia lancinante de un enigma
que ha de quedar sin respuesta para siempre.

keeps trying to decipher all in vain.
Moss spreads on the floor
the slippery carpet
of an abandoned sepulcher.
In between the wind and his wakefulness
starts up the sudden certainty
that this feeble adventure is another instance
of the shifting of fortune that has muddied over
each moment of his life.
Even the matchless monument of his work
dissolves away and loses utterly
all justification, argument, and meaning.
To return to nothing draws him with the feeling
of relief, a secret and assuaging balm
that the gods offer in compassion.
The voice of the wind brings in
the anxious cry which summons him
from that other shore where time holds no dominion
nor exercises any power
with all its bitter plots and machinations.
The north wind moves away, the wind falls silent
and a stifled cry chokes in his sleepless throat.
The silence is answered by another silence,
his silence, habitual silence, the same silence
from which will still spill out, for a brief spell,
the graceful wellspring of his music
like no other music, which hands on to us
the piercing nostalgia of an enigma
that must remain unanswered for all time.

[A.R.]

Cita

Para Eulalio and Rafaela

Camino de Salamanca. El verano
establece sobre Castilla su luz abrasadora.
El autobús espera para arreglar una avería
en un pueblo cuyo nombre ya he olvidado.
Me interno por callejas donde el tórrido
silencio deshace el tiempo en el atónito polvo
que cruza el aire con mansa parsimonia.
El empedrado corredor de una fonda
me invita con su sombra a refugiarme
en sus arcadas. Entro. La sala está vacía,
nadie en el pequeño jardín cuya frescura
se esparce desde el tazón de piedra
de la fuente hasta la humilde penumbra
de los aposentos. Por un estrecho pasillo
desemboco en un corral ruinoso
que me devuelve al tiempo de las diligencias.
Entre la tierra del piso sobresale
lo que antes fuera el brocal de un pozo.
De repente, en medio del silencio,
bajo el resplandor intacto del verano,
lo veo velar sus armas, meditar abstraído
y de sus ojos tristes demorar la mirada
en este intruso que, sin medir sus pasos,
ha llegado hasta él desde esas Indias
de las que tiene una vaga noticia.
Por el camino he venido recordando, recreando
sus hechos mientras cruzábamos las tierras labrantías.
Lo tuve tan presente, tan cercano,
que ahora que lo encuentro me parece
que se trata de una cita urdida
con minuciosa paciencia en tantos años

Appointment

For Eulalio and Rafaela

On the way to Salamanca. Summer
affirms its blazing light over Castile.
The bus awaits repair in a village
whose name I have already forgotten.
I venture into narrow streets where scorching
silence reduces time to stunned dust
drifting through the air at its gentle leisure.
The shade of a paved hallway
invites me to shelter in the arcades
of an inn. I enter. The lounge is empty;
no one in the small garden whose coolness
flows out from the stone bowl
of the fountain to the modest obscurity
of the rooms. From a narrow passage
I step into a rundown yard
that sends me back to the era of coaches.
What must once have been a well's parapet
rises from the earthen floor.
Suddenly, in the midst of silence,
beneath the unblemished radiance of summer,
I see him watching over his arms, lost in thought,
letting the gaze of his sad eyes linger
on this intruder who has come to him
with reckless tread from those Indies
of which he has heard some vague report.
On the way, as we crossed the farmlands,
I was recalling, recreating his deeds.
He was so close, so much in my thoughts,
that the encounter with him now
feels like an appointment planned
with meticulous patience over all the years

de fervor sin tregua por este Caballero
de la Triste Figura, por su lección
que ha de durar lo que duren los hombres,
por su vigilia poblada de improbables
hazañas que son nuestro pan de cada día.
No debo interrumpir su dolorido velar
en este pozo cegado por la mísera incuria
de los hombres. Me retiro. Recorro una vez más
las callejas de este pueblo castellano
y a nadie participo del encuentro.
En una hora estaremos en Alba de Tormes.
¿Cómo hace España para albergar tanta impaciente savia
que sostiene el desolado insistir de nuestra vida,
tanta obstinada sangre para amar y morir según enseña
el rendido amador de Dulcinea?

of my unflagging fervor for this Knight
of the Sad Countenance, for his lesson
which will last as long as humanity,
for his vigil thronged with the unlikely
feats that are our daily bread.
I should not disturb his sorrowful watch
at this well blocked by wretched neglect.
I withdraw. I walk the narrow streets
of this Castilian village once again
and tell no one of my encounter.
In an hour we will be in Alba de Tormes.
How is it Spain holds so much eager sap
that feeds the bleak persistence of our life,
so much stubborn blood for loving and dying
by the word of Dulcinea's gallant vassal?

[C.A.]

Celebración de la vid

Canto la vid, su hoja de cinco puntas
que copia la mano del hombre.
Alabo su terca fidelidad
al ingrato suelo que la acoge.
Celebro su condición de testigo:
compañera de Platón, hermana de Omar Khayam,
señora de los jardines de Córdoba
en donde los Omeyas exaltaron el álgebra y la vida.
Reclamo para la vid el homenaje sin pausa
que le deben nuestra sangre y la persistencia
mineral de nuestros huesos, resignado limo del subsuelo.
Allí tornamos a encontrarnos con ella
y desde sus raíces volvemos a la vida
hechos sol y sabias mieles vegetales,
presentes en la uva para vivir
un fugaz instante de la eternidad.
Proclamo para la vid la fervorosa simpatía
de los hombres que le deben el canto y las batallas,
la oración y la lenta agonía del saber.
Así sea.

Celebration of the Vine

I sing the vine, its five-pointed leaf
that copies the human hand.
I praise its stubborn fidelity
to the haggard soil that receives it.
I celebrate its role as witness:
companion to Plato, sister to Omar Khayyám,
mistress of the gardens of Córdoba
where the Umayyads glorified algebra and life.
I call for the ceaseless homage to the vine
owed by our blood and the mineral persistence
of our bones, resigned to nourishing the subsoil.
There we return to meet with the vine
and through its roots come back to life
transformed into sunlight and sapient nectars,
gathered in the grape to live
a fleeting moment of the eternal.
I proclaim our fervent sympathy
for the vine to which we owe song and battles,
prayer and the slow agony of knowledge.
So be it.

[C.A.]

Como espadas en desorden

Mínimo homenaje a Stéphane Mallarmé

Como espadas en desorden
la luz recorre los campos.
Islas de sombra se desvanecen
e intentan, en vano, sobrevivir más lejos.
Allí, de nuevo, las alcanza el fulgor
del mediodía que ordena sus huestes
y establece sus dominios.
El hombre nada sabe de estos callados combates.
Su vocación de penumbra, su costumbre de olvido,
sus hábitos, en fin, y sus lacerias,
le niegan el goce de esa fiesta imprevista
que sucede por caprichoso designio
de quienes, en lo alto, lanzan los mudos dados
cuya cifra jamás conoceremos.
Los sabios, entretanto, predican la conformidad.
Sólo los dioses saben que esta virtud incierta
es otro vano intento de abolir el azar.

Like Swords in Disarray

Little homage to Stéphane Mallarmé

Like swords in disarray
light scours the countryside.
Islands of shadow, dispersed, attempt
in vain to hold out farther afield,
there, again, to be found by the radiance
of midday marshalling its hosts,
imposing its rule.
Mankind knows nothing of these tacit battles.
Our bent for half-light, our custom of forgetting,
our habits, in short, and our penuries
bar us from that unforeseen fiesta
held at the capricious decree
of those who, on high, cast the mute dice
whose sum we shall never learn.
The wise, meanwhile, counsel conformity.
That dubious virtue, the gods only know,
is one more vain attempt to cancel chance.

[C.A.]

Si oyes correr el agua

Si oyes correr el agua en las acequias,
su manso sueño pasar entre penumbras y musgos,
con el apagado sonido de algo
que tiende a demorarse en la sombra vegetal.
Si tienes suerte y preservas ese instante
con el temblor de los helechos que no cesa,
con el atónito limo que se debate
en el cauce inmutable y siempre en viaje.
Si tienes la paciencia del guijarro,
su voz callada, su gris acento sin aristas,
y aguardas hasta que la luz haga su entrada,
es bueno que sepas que allí van a llamarte
con un nombre nunca antes pronunciado.
Toda la ardua armonía del mundo
es probable que entonces te sea revelada,
pero sólo por esta vez.
¡Sabrás, acaso, descifrarla en el rumor del agua
que se evade sin remedio y para siempre?

If You Hear the Water Flow

If you hear the water flow in the channels,
its calm dream passing among glooms and mosses
with the muffled sound of something
inclined to linger in the shade of plants.
If you are lucky and hold on to that moment
with its continual trembling of ferns,
with its stunned silt that wrestles
in the changeless, ever-shifting bed.
If you have the patience of a pebble,
its quiet voice, its smooth, gray accent,
and wait for the light to make its entrance,
you should know that there you will be called
by a name never yet pronounced.
All the world's arduous harmony
may well be revealed to you then
but for that one time only.
Will you by chance know how to discern it
in the murmur of the water as it slips
away irrecoverably forever?

[C.A.]

Visita de la lluvia

Para Vicente Rojo

Ocurre así la lluvia.
   —Aurelio Arturo

Llega de repente la lluvia, instala sus huestes, minuciosos
guerreros de seda y sueño.

Salta gozosa en los tejados, desciende por los canalones
en precipitada algarabía;

comienza la gran fiesta de las aguas en viaje que establ-
ecen su transitorio dominio

y de la mano nos llevan a regiones que el tiempo había
sepultado, al parecer, para siempre:

allí nos esperan

la fiebre de la infancia,

la lenta convalecencia en tardes de un otoño incesante,

los amores que se prometían sin término,

los duelos en la familia,

los húmedos funerales en el campo,

el tren detenido ante el viaducto que arrastró la
creciente,

los insectos zumbando en el vagón donde nos sorprendió
el alba,

las historias de piratas codiciosos, de malayos que
degüellan en silencio, de viajes al polo, de tormentas
devastadoras e islas afortunadas;

nuestros padres, jóvenes, mucho más jóvenes que
nosotros ahora, que la lluvia rescata de su parda ceniza sin
edad, de su callado trabajo mineral

e irrumpen vestidos de risa y gestos juveniles.

Qué bendición la lluvia, que intacta maravilla su paso
sorpresivo y bienhechor

que nos preserva del olvido y de la mansa rutina sin
memoria.

Visiting Rain

For Vicente Rojo

"This is how the rain happens."
—Aurelio Arturo

Suddenly the rain arrives, deploying its hosts, miniature
warriors of silk and dream.

Gleefully it jumps on the roofs, rushes down the
gutters in precipitous jubilation;

so begins the great festival of traveling waters, impos-
ing their transitory rule,

leading us by the hand to regions that time had buried,
it seemed, forever:

Childhood fever

awaits us there

and slow convalescence in afternoons of an autumn
without end,

loves declared eternal,

deaths in the family,

humid country funerals,

the train come to a halt before the viaduct swept away
by the flood,

insects buzzing in the railway car where daybreak
found us,

stories of rapacious pirates, Malays quietly slitting
throats, journeys to the Pole, devastating storms, and
fortunate isles;

our parents in their youth, far younger than we are
now, salvaged by the rain from their dun, ageless ash, their
hushed elemental toil;

in they burst, clothed in laughter and boisterous
gestures.

What a blessing the rain is, what an unspoiled wonder
its surprising, salutary passage

Con qué gozo transparente nos instalamos en su
imperio de palios vegetales

y con cuánta construida resignación la escuchamos
callar pausadamente, alejarse y regresar por un un in-
stante,

hasta que nos abandona en medio de un lavado silencio,
de un ámbito recién inaugurado

que invade el presente con sus turbias materias en
derrota, su cortejo de pálidas convicciones, de costumbres
donde no cabe la esperanza.

Recordemos siempre esta visita de la lluvia. Cerrados
los ojos, tratemos de evocar su vocerío

y asistamos de nuevo a la victoria de sus huestes que,
por un instante, derrotan a la muerte.

which saves us from forgetting and the tranquil amnesiac routine.

We settle with such transparent joy in its empire of plant canopies

and listen with such composed resignation as gradually it falls silent, withdraws, and returns for a moment,

before leaving us at the heart of a washed silence, a freshly inaugurated space

which the present invades with its murky perishables, its retinue of bloodless convictions and habits that leave no room for hope.

Let us always remember this visiting rain. With eyes shut, let us try to summon its clamor

and witness once again the triumph of its hosts as they prevail, for a moment, over death.

[C.A.]

Pienso a veces . . .

Para Alejandro Rossi

Pienso a veces que ha llegado la hora de callar.
Dejar a un lado las palabras,
las pobres palabras usadas
hasta sus últimas cuerdas,
vejadas una y otra vez
hasta haber perdido
el más leve signo
de su original intención
de nombrar las cosas, los seres,
los paisajes, los ríos
y las efímeras pasiones de los hombres
montados en sus corceles
que atavió la vanidad
antes de recibir la escueta,
la irrebatible lección de la tumba.

Siempre los mismos,
gastando las palabras
hasta no poder, siquiera, orar con ellos,
ni exhibir sus deseos
en la parca extensión de sus sueños,
sus mendicantes sueños,
más propicios a la piedad y al olvido
que al vano estertor de la memoria.

Las palabras, en fin, cayendo
al pozo sin fondo
donde van a buscarlas
los infatuados tribunos
ávidos de un poder
hecho de sombra y desventura.

There Are Days When I Think . . .

For Alejandro Rossi

There are days when I think the time has come to be quiet.
To set words aside,
poor words worn
threadbare,
abused over and again
until not the faintest
trace is left
of their original purpose:
the naming of things, beings,
landscapes, rivers,
and the transient passions of men and women
mounted on steeds
that vanity adorned
before it was dealt the succinct
and irrefutable lesson of the tomb.

People forever
wearing out words
until they no longer serve even for prayer
or the display of desire
within the meager compass of dreams,
mendicant dreams,
fitter for mercy and forgetting
than for the vain death rattle of memory.

Words falling finally
into the bottomless well,
there to be sought
by fatuous tribunes
thirsting for a power
made of shadow and trouble.

Inmerso en el silencio,
sumergido en sus aguas tranquilas
de acequia que detiene su curso
y se entrega al inmóvil
sosiego de las lianas,
al imperceptible palpitar de las raíces;
en el silencio, ya lo dijo Rimbaud,
ha de morar el poema,
el único posible ya,
labrado en los abismos
en donde todo lo nombrado
perdió hace mucho tiempo
la menor ocasión de subsistir,
de instaurar su estéril mentira
tejida en la rala trama de las palabras
que giran sin sosiego en el vacío
donde van a perderse
las necias tareas de los hombres.
Pienso a veces que ha llegado la hora de callar,
pero el silencio sería entonces
un premio desmedido,
una gracia inefable
que no creo haber ganado todavía.

Immersed in silence,
submerged in its calm waters
like those of a channel that stops its flow
and yields to the still
tranquility of lianas,
to the imperceptible pulsing of roots,
in silence, as Rimbaud said, the poem
must dwell, the only
poem still possible,
forged in the abysses
where all that is named
has long since lost
the least chance of survival,
of establishing its sterile lie
woven into the scanty fabric of words
which spin on and on
in the void that will swallow
the foolish assignments of mankind.
There are days when I think the time has come to be quiet,
but silence then would be
an inordinate prize,
an ineffable grace
that I do not believe I have yet earned.

[C.A.]

DANTE ALIGHIERI THE NEW LIFE
Translated by Dante Gabriel Rossetti; Preface by Michael Palmer

KINGSLEY AMIS COLLECTED POEMS: 1944–1979

ANTONELLA ANEDDA HISTORIAE
Translated by Patrizio Ceccagnoli and Susan Stewart

GUILLAUME APOLLINAIRE ZONE: SELECTED POEMS
Translated by Ron Padgett

AUSTERITY MEASURES THE NEW GREEK POETRY
Edited by Karen Van Dyck

SZILÁRD BORBÉLY BERLIN-HAMLET
Translated by Ottilie Mulzet

SZILÁRD BORBÉLY IN A BUCOLIC LAND
Translated by Ottilie Mulzet

ANDRÉ BRETON AND PHILIPPE SOUPAULT THE MAGNETIC
FIELDS
Translated by Charlotte Mandel

MARGARET CAVENDISH *Edited by Michael Robbins*

AMIT CHAUDHURI Sweet Shop: New and Selected Poems, 1985–202

NAJWAN DARWISH EXHAUSTED ON THE CROSS
Translated by Kareem James Abu-Zeid; Foreword by Raúl Zurita

NAJWAN DARWISH NOTHING MORE TO LOSE
Translated by Kareem James Abu-Zeid

BENJAMIN FONDANE CINEPOEMS AND OTHERS
Edited by Leonard Schwartz

GLORIA GERVITZ MIGRATIONS: POEM, 1976–2020